Politics and the Other Scene

V

PHRONESIS

A series from Verso edited by
Ernesto Laclau and Chantal Mouffe

Since 1989, when the first Phronesis book was published, many events of fundamental importance to the series have taken place. Some of them initially brought the hope that great possibilities were opening up for the extension and deepening of democracy, one of the main points of focus in our reflections. Disenchantment, however, came quickly and what we witnessed instead was the reinforcement and generalization of the neoliberal hegemony. Today, the left-wing project is in an even deeper crisis than it was ten years ago. An increasing number of social-democratic parties, under the pretence of 'modernizing' themselves, are discarding their Left identity. According to the advocates of the 'third way', and with the advent of globalization, the time has come to abandon the old dogmas of Left and Right and promote a new entrepreneurial spirit at all levels of society.

Phronesis's objective is to establish a dialogue among all those who assert the need to redefine the Left/Right distinction – which constitutes the crucial dynamic of modern democracy – instead of relinquishing it. Our original concern, which was to bring together left-wing politics and the theoretical developments around the critique of essentialism, is more pertinent than ever. Indeed, we still believe that the most important trends in contemporary theory – deconstruction, psychoanalysis, the philosophy of language as initiated by the later Wittgenstein and post-Heideggerian hermeneutics – are the necessary conditions for understanding the widening of social struggles characteristic of the present stage of democratic politics, and for formulating a new vision for the Left in terms of radical and plural democracy.

Politics and the Other Scene

ÉTIENNE BALIBAR

Translations by Christine Jones,
James Swenson, Chris Turner

VERSO
London • New York

This edition first published by Verso 2002

© Verso 2002

Introduction © Étienne Balibar 2002

Translations © Christine Jones, James Swenson, Chris Turner 2002

First published as chapters in *La Crainte des masses:*
Politique et philosophie avant et après Marx © Editions Galilée 1997
and *Droit de cité: Culture et politique en démocratie,*
© Editions de l'Aube 1998

All rights reserved

The moral rights of the author and the translators have been asserted

1 3 5 7 9 10 8 6 4 2

Verso
UK: 6 Meard Street, London W1F 0EG
USA: 180 Varick Street, New York, NY 10014–4606
www.versobooks.com

Verso is the imprint of New Left Books

ISBN 1–85984–725–0
ISBN 1–85984–267–4 (pbk)

British Library Cataloguing in Publication Data
A catalogue record for this book is available from the British Library

Library of Congress Cataloging-in-Publication Data
A catalog record for this book is available from the Library of Congress

Typeset in 10 on 12 ITC New Baskerville by
SetSystems Ltd, Saffron Walden, Essex
Printed by Biddles Ltd, Guildford and Kings Lynn
www.biddles.co.uk

Contents

Preface

The essays collected in this book have already appeared in French, albeit in a different form. So in one sense it is a new book; and in another it is an old one. This creates a certain difficulty in presenting it, for which I ask the reader's indulgence. I shall briefly explain how this came about, hoping that I will be forgiven for going into some detail about my publications in both languages. I will then proceed to summarize what I regard as the principal themes of the book, and how I would define the main thread that connects them. Finally, I shall say a few words about the conception of politics that I wanted to introduce by borrowing the metaphor of the 'other scene' from Freud.

Most of the essays below derive from a collection published in France entitled 'Fear of the Masses: Politics and Philosophy before and after Marx'.[1] They formed its general introduction ('Three Concepts of Politics'); its third part (already presented under the subtitle: 'The Other Scene: Violence, Borders, Universality'); and its general conclusion ('Ambiguous Universality'). Only one of them ('Is a European Citizenship Possible?') comes from another collection.[2] Some, however, were adapted from papers or lectures originally delivered in English. And the French volume was itself an expanded version of the book *Masses, Classes, Ideas: Studies in Politics and Philosophy before and after Marx*, published by Routledge in 1993. It was my friend John Rajchman who generously suggested that I should collect some of my more recent essays, so as to indicate to

an Anglophone readership how I thought a critical reading of Marx
and Marxist theory (along lines initiated many years ago in collaboration with Althusser) could be combined with other interpretations
of the tradition of political philosophy (Spinoza, Rousseau, Kant,
Fichte), and above all with contributions to contemporary debates
about universalism, racism, nationalism, and citizenship – more
generally, what I called a 'politics of the Rights of Man' (deliberately
adopting, in spite of its obvious 'male chauvinist' bias, the terminology of the Enlightenment and the 'Declarations' in which the
principle of 'equal liberty' is expressed[3]). By the time I realized that
a similar collection might also be useful in French, and I could
devote some effort to its preparation, time had already passed,
during which there had been occasion enough to discuss the
political and philosophical questions involved in 'identity politics'.
The result was a considerable expansion of the horizons of the
American volume. Consequently, I thought it necessary to reorgan-
ize its contents by adding new material, and a general introduction.

It was this circumstance that led Ernesto Laclau, Chantal Mouffe
and Verso to suggest that the return journey should be also
attempted – that is, transmitting the new material to an English
readership. For this I want to express my deepest gratitude. But
while I accepted their suggestion, I persuaded myself (and want to
try to persuade my new readers) that the resulting volume is not a
mere sequel or supplement to *Masses, Classes, Ideas*, but has a unity
of its own: a problematic – if not a single – object. To be sure, some
of the presuppositions of my arguments have been unpacked, but
they can be found in several existing volumes: *Masses, Classes, Ideas*,
but also *Spinoza and Politics* (Verso), plus *Race, Nation, Class* (written
with Immanuel Wallerstein) (Verso), and *The Philosophy of Marx*
(Verso). And I take the opportunity to focus the attention on what
I consider to be a major problem: the aporias of a reduction of
extreme violence, which led me to suggest in my introductory essay
that the two critical concepts which continue to inspire much
political philosophy in the progressive tradition (*emancipation* and
transformation) should be rounded off (but certainly not replaced)
by a third one, for which I borrowed the old concept of *civility*.[4]

Approaching things from a rather formal angle, it might be said that the combination of issues that underlies my essays, and provides them with a certain continuity (there is no question of claiming that they are the *only* issues of political philosophy, but I would reject any suggestion that they are marginal), emerges from a comparison between two titles that end with a question mark – 'Is There Such a Thing as European Racism?', 'Is a European Citizenship Possible?' – and two notions that are said to be 'ambiguous': Identities and Universality.

This book was written at a time when imparting an actual content to the notion of a 'European Citizenship' became urgent quite independently of the merely juridical point of how the future 'constitution' of Europe should be labelled. The issue is to decide what kind of status and rights (*civil, political and social,* to follow a famous tripartition that retains its relevance) the inhabitants of this new political entity would individually and collectively enjoy. They can mark either an advance or a regression in the history of citizenship; and this has not yet been settled. But the book was also written while the various manifestations of institutional and ideological racism were acquiring their present configuration, which I ventured to describe as a potential 'European apartheid': the dark side, as it were, of the emergence of the 'European citizen'. It involves a rampant repression of 'alien' communities of immigrants (with specific modalities progressively unified under the Schengen Convention); a diffusion among European nations of openly racist outbursts (neo-fascist or 'populist' propaganda and activities, pogroms, expulsions on a massive scale); and a seemingly contradictory combination of nationalist exclusivism and 'Western' communitarianism.

I have two main theses on this point. One is that a new definition of citizenship in Europe can only be the definition of a new citizenship. It must become *more* democratic than the old 'national-social' form of citizenship used to be, or it will become less so – and is bound to fail. There can and will be no status quo. In particular, the construction of citizenship in Europe will either include *all the communities that are historically present* on European territory; or it will mean a defeat for the ideal of universality that nation-states embodied to a certain extent (because they were pushed by two centuries of class struggle and other democratic movements), and which enabled them to secure popular consent. But such a crossroads poses a problem that is simultaneously very speculative in its formulation and very concrete in its implications: the problem of the *community*, or the *mode of identification* that gives rise to the representation of a community. 'Community' and 'citizenship' have had a problematic relationship since the origins of political thought. (The Greeks had only one word to express these two aspects: *politeia*, whence we derive our 'politics' as well as our 'police'. But this meant that the contradictions were located *within* this single concept, and conferred on it an immediately 'dialectical' meaning.) I defend the idea that the contradictory nature of the notion of political community (which requires both unity and diversity, conflict and consent, integration and exclusion, substantial identity and openness to indefinite change) reflects a tension not only between the real and the ideal, or between different 'imagined communities', but also between *the self-assertion and deconstruction of community as such* – or the opposite requirements of 'identification' and 'disidentification'. My thesis is that democratic politics is a difficult, 'ambiguous' art of combining the opposed terms of identification and disidentification (including *identification with the universal*), and for that reason it remains permanently exposed to turning into its opposite.

But these dilemmas are not presented to us in an indeterminate and neutral context. The conjuncture of the break-up of Yugoslavia and its tragic aftermath; the analogy between tendencies towards a 'European apartheid' and the phenomenon of 'ethnic cleansing' that Europeans too easily imagine is typical of the 'underdeveloped' world; above all, the fact that such ultra-subjective or *idealistic* forms of violence are never *concretely* isolated from quite different forms which may also lead to processes of extermination (economic violence in which the social causes do not take the form of human agency, but are naturalized and fetishized, to use Marxist terminology) – these led me to take a special interest in the question of *borders* and their current transformation. What I attempted here is actually only a sketch open to debate, lacking as it does the requisite historical, anthropological and sociological precision. But while it connects the issues of identity, community, citizenship and social policy in a single complex, which constitutes *the internal condition of a permanent reconstitution of political practice*, the problem of borders is also intended as a metonymy of how politics can be related to the now inescapable issue of *globalization*. Borders (including 'internal' borders) are 'global' *per se*: they are projections of the world (dis)order; and the kind of violence that concentrates on their more or less stable lines, notwithstanding its 'local' and 'specific' roots and forms, is widely supposed to form a counterpart to globalization. At the very least, it becomes integrated into an expanding economy of global violence, thus posing the question as to whether a globalization of politics can also mean a politics of globalization.

There is no question here of entering into the debates on globalization (more than I actually do in the book) – not even to discuss whether the term is acceptable and, if so, in what sense. I shall jump to a speculative consideration, which derives from my focus on the relationship between politics and violence as illustrated by the operation of the 'border' – the non-democratic condition of democracy itself, as it were. Let me express it allegorically by saying that the 'global' system, which tends to be pictured in *Hobbesian* terms (as a *war of all against all* based on interests, powers, cultures, etc., requiring a regulation through either law or force, or rather a close combination of the two), is in reality profoundly *anti-Hobbesian*. This is so because it is no longer possible to regard the phenomenon of violence within itself as a 'state of nature', that is, as a structural condition that *precedes institutions (civil, political)*, and which institutions as such would suppress. We have had to accept (particularly after the experiences of revolution and counter-revolution, fascism and anti-fascism, de-colonization and neocolonialism, the emergence of the neoliberal 'empire' and its opponents) that extreme violence is not post-historical but actually 'post-institutional'. Extreme violence arises from institutions as much as it arises against them, and it is not possible to escape this circle by 'absolute' decisions such as choosing between a violent or a non-violent politics, or between force and law. The only 'way' out of the circle is to invent a *politics of violence*, or to *introduce the issue of violence*, its forms and limits, its regulation and perverse effects on agents themselves, *into the concept and practice of politics* (whereas, traditionally, the 'essence' of politics was either represented as the absolute negation of violence, or identified with its 'legitimate' use). In particular, it means introducing the issue of violence and a strategy of anti-violence into emancipatory politics itself, which has led me to suggest elsewhere that 'civilizing the revolution' might be a precondition for 'civilizing the state'.

A politics of violence, or a politics of civility (the same thing obversely formulated), is not something that can be pursued solely on the *stage* of globalization, where processes, motivations and interests are supposed to be visible and manageable. However conflictual or antagonistic, globalization tends to represent itself as a homogeneous process that combines *given agencies* (initially economic forces, but also increasingly ideological ones) into a single system of interactions. Yet when we have to deal with what makes its evolution unpredictable and possibly unintelligible, ghosts, devils and virtual forces are not slow to make their entry. It was to help escape this dilemma, which I found intolerable, that I sought an analogy in the Freudian notion of 'the other scene'.

Freud uses this expression (which comes from Fechner) several times, notably in *The Interpretation of Dreams*. It contributes to a model of the 'mental apparatus' in which processes of repression of desire and the return of the repressed in 'regressive' form can be 'located' and dynamically assembled.[5] Drawing on this representation of the *essential heterogeneity* of psychic processes to express the no less essential heterogeneity of political processes affords several possibilities, which I can only briefly indicate here.

A first possibility would be to draw attention to the amount of information that is either structurally inaccessible to, or deliberately concealed from, collective agents on the world stage. It is merely a seeming paradox that this phenomenon has progressed enormously in the 'information age', when the dominant powers have learnt to replace the old practice of secrecy [*arcana imperii*] by the manipulation of mass information (in which they, too, sometimes become entrapped). Here, the 'other scene' would mean that crucial determinants of our own action remain invisible in the very forms of (tele)visibility, whereas we urgently require them to assess the conjuncture or 'take sides' in conflicts where it is possible neither simply to attribute the labels of justice and injustice, nor to rise 'above the fray' in the name of some superior determination of history. Although this is not the precise sense in which I want to develop the idea, I by no means exclude it, if only because it offers us a direct transition to the idea that the *other scene* of politics is also *the scene of the other*, where the visible–incomprehensible victims and enemies are located at the level of fantasy. Secrecy, counter-information and fantasmatic otherness must have some common root; at least they produce conjoint effects.

But the 'other scene' could also mean something more abstract, which restores an essential pattern of historical explanation. In a sense, drawing attention to the other scene and indicating its capacity to determine the course of historical events was exactly what Marx was doing when he urged revolutionaries and, more generally, rational minds to turn away from the 'apparent scene' of politics, structured by discourses and ideas/ideals, and *unveil* the 'real scene' of economic processes, the development of capitalism and class struggle. As readers may notice, I have a certain tendency to *invert this pattern* – not to return to the idea that 'ideas drive history', but to emphasize the fact that 'material' processes are themselves (over- and under-) determined by the processes of the imaginary, which have their own very effective materiality and need to be unveiled. I have, as it were, made the imaginary the 'infrastructure of the infrastructure' itself, starting with the idea that all forces which interact in the economico-political realm are also collective groupings, and consequently possess an (ambivalent) imaginary identity. In this way, I have implicitly suggested that recognition of the other scene is theoretically associated with the rejection, not of class antagonisms and the structure of capitalism, but of an absolute 'last instance', and with the adoption of a *broad* (hence heterogeneous) concept of materiality. But I have also run the risk of purely and simply identifying the political other scene with the scene of imaginary collective processes and their unconscious determinants. This is not exactly what I want to suggest here. The other scene that emerges with the conjunction of several forms of extreme violence, such as absolute mass impoverishment and suicidal or exterminist policies, is no more an *ideological-imaginary* than an *economico-social* scene: it precisely involves an interference of their respective logics and their 'normal' institutional articulation, producing an effect of strangeness and a disruption of subjectivities.

What I call the other scene (perhaps I should also say the *other scenario*) is thus not so much a concrete or theoretical place, although distinct places are necessary for its constitution, as the *moment* where it *becomes manifest* that politics is not 'rational' (but is not simply 'irrational' either): particularly because both institutions and counter-institutions (without which there is no collective practice, but also no individual life) include the permanent possibility of destruction and self-destruction. Death drives are involved here, but so are other forms of the 'negative' that ought to be reckoned worse than death, or that engage history in regressive processes (such as the 'necessity' for capitalism to neutralize and eliminate whole populations rather than including them in productive processes that would also increase their capacity for resistance and political struggle); or in 'traumatic' repetitions (such as the transformation of victims or their descendants into executioners, and the endless cycle of attack and retaliation that the New World Order seems to set in train). At such a time, the necessity of reconstituting political practices confronts more difficulties and uncertainties. But the meaning of collective agency is enhanced rather than diminished, because it faces additional tasks, such as inventing new ideas of community that have no guarantee of being 'just', or – as I said above – civilizing the revolution in order to civilize the state. Thus such a political practice not only demands commitment, intelligence and effort. It seems to involve a tragic dimension, deriving from the fact that men and women set themselves goals that they are never certain will not destroy them, while they are precisely struggling against annihilation. 'Pessimism of the intelligence, optimism of the will', as Gramsci wrote. Another name for *phronesis*? I leave it to the editors to decide.

Irvine, 19 January 2002

Notes

1. *La Crainte des masses. Politique et philosophie avant et après Marx.* Paris: Galilée 1997.
2. *Droit de cité. Culture et politique en démocratie.* La Tour d'Aigues: Editions de l'Aube 1998.
3. In a deliberate play on words, I called it *égaliberté*, which is not really translatable.
4. All the essays in this book were written before '11 September', and I have not changed a word in them. Or – to take up a highly pertinent suggestion by Immanuel Wallerstein (in his Charles R. Lawrence II Memorial Lecture, Brooklyn College, 5 December 2001: 'America and the World: The Twin Towers as Metaphors') – they were written between two dates whose 'coincidence' represents an amazing symbol: 11 September 1973 (the Pinochet coup in Chile, seemingly prepared in close co-operation with the US government, with thousands of victims) and 11 September 2001 (the destruction of the World Trade Center in Manhattan, apparently prepared by a secret terrorist organization rooted in Saudi Arabia and other Islamic countries, with thousands of victims).
5. See *The Standard Edition of the Complete Psychological Works of Sigmund Freud,* London 1958, vol. V, pp. 535 ff.

1

Three Concepts of Politics: Emancipation, Transformation, Civility

When it comes to thinking about politics (and how can we act politically without thinking about politics?), I believe we cannot get by without at least three distinct concepts which connect together in problematic fashion. This dialectic (it is a dialectic, even if it does not include any final synthesis) is not the only one conceivable. The names and figures to which it will refer could be referred to differently. They are provisional, and tend only to mark out certain differences. But the principle itself seems to me inescapable.

I shall attempt to characterize these concepts from a logical and an ethical point of view, referring on each occasion to typical formulations, and outlining some of the problems they raise. I shall call the first concept the *autonomy of politics*, and I shall link this with the ethical figure of *emancipation*. By contrast, I shall call the second concept the *heteronomy of politics*, or politics related to structural and conjunctural *conditions*, and I shall connect this to the figures (we shall see that these are themselves multiple) of *transformation*. It will then be necessary to introduce – on the basis of certain aporias of the second concept, but as a new figure in its own right – a concept I shall call the *heteronomy of heteronomy*, as this will show that the conditions to which a politics relates are never a last instance: on the contrary, what makes them determinant is the way they bear subjects or are borne by them. Now, subjects act in accordance with the identity which is imposed on them or which they create for themselves. The imaginary dimension in which identities are shaped, and senses of belonging formed and unformed, is, then, the condition of conditions; it is, as it were, the 'other scene' on which the effects of the autonomy and heteronomy of politics are engineered. Corresponding to this there is, also, a politics, which is irreducible either to emancipation or to transformation, the ethical horizon of which I shall characterize as *civility*.

Autonomy of Politics: Emancipation

The autonomy of politics is not the autonomy of *the political*. It is not a matter either of isolating the sphere of power and institutions, or of making room in the celestial realm of ideas for the essence of the community. It is a question, rather, of understanding how politics defines itself when it refers to a *de jure* universality which we may term *intensive*,[1] because it expresses the principle, declared or undeclared, that the community (the 'people', the 'nation', the 'society', the 'state', but also the 'international community' or 'humanity') cannot exist as such, nor govern itself, so long as it is based on the subjection of its members to a natural or transcendent authority, and on the establishment of constraint and discrimination.

Elsewhere, drawing on what is clearly not the only statement of politics understood in this sense, but certainly one of the most decisive (the *Declaration of the Rights of Man and the Citizen* [1789]), I suggested giving the name the 'proposition of equaliberty'[2] to the generic formulation in which the two – practically inseparable – sides of this proclamation of autonomy are combined: no equality without liberty, no liberty without equality. It is certain that the revolutions termed bourgeois (which were not very bourgeois at all in the moment of insurrection against despotism and privilege, the moment Negri calls 'constituent'[3]) gave a very particular force to that proclamation by linking it to an ideology of a return to lost (natural and rational) origins.[4] There is, however, no reason to think either that it belongs exclusively to them, or that the regimes and states arising out of that declaration, which have enshrined its principles in their constitutions, are those which best preserve its symbolic and practical effectiveness.

Why should we consider that we have here a typical formulation of the autonomy of politics – a formulation the truth of which we still have to acknowledge today, while at the same time assessing the difficulties which go with it? It seems to me that we should do so for two, mutually supportive, reasons. The proposition of equal liberty, as stated in revolutionary terms,[5] has a remarkable logical form which has, since the Greeks, been termed an *elegkhos* or, in other words, a self-refutation of its negation. It states the fact that it is *impossible* to maintain to a logical conclusion, without absurdity, the idea of perfect civil liberty based on discrimination, privilege and inequalities of condition (and, *a fortiori*, to institute such liberty), just as it is impossible to conceive and institute equality between human beings based on despotism (even 'enlightened' despotism) or on a monopoly of power. Equal liberty is, therefore, *unconditional.* This finds more concrete expression in two consequences.

The first is that politics is an unfolding of the self-determination of the people [*demos*] (if we give this generic name to the body of citizens 'free and equal in rights'), which constitutes itself in and by the establishment of its rights. Whatever the conditions in which individuals, communities or collectivities capable of recognizing each other as political subjects find themselves, and whatever the causes of the restrictions imposed on liberty and equality, those restrictions are in themselves illegitimate: their abolition may be demanded immediately. In the deepest interpretation of this situation, it is not so much a question of removing an oppressive external power as of *suppressing that which separates the people from itself* (from its own autonomy). This generation or regeneration of the people is, at least, the precondition for its 'winning democracy' in the face of any form of domination. It is, therefore, the people's own responsibility, as Kant was to put it in a famous text inspired by Saint Paul.[6] Hence the close affinity which, throughout history (at least Western history), unites the politics of autonomy to the philosophical principles of Natural Right.

However, the unconditional form of the proposition entails yet another necessary consequence, which we may call the *reciprocity clause.* I shall express this by saying that such a proposition implies a universal right to politics. No one may be liberated or elevated to a position of equality – let us say, may *be emancipated* – by an external, unilateral decision, or by a higher grace. Only reciprocally, by mutual recognition, can this be achieved. The rights which form the content of equal liberty, and lend it material form, are, by definition, individual rights, rights of persons. However, since they cannot be granted, they have to be won, and they can be won only collectively. It is of their essence to be rights individuals confer upon each other, guarantee to one another.[7] In this way, we move from the self-determination of the people to the autonomy of politics itself. The autonomy of politics (in so far as it represents a process that has its origin and its end in itself alone, or in what will be termed citizenship) is not conceivable without the autonomy of its subject, and this in turn is nothing other than the fact, for the people, that it 'makes' itself, at the same time as the individuals who constitute the people confer basic rights upon one another mutually. There is autonomy of politics only to the extent that subjects are the source and ultimate reference of emancipation for each other.

The subjects of politics understood in this sense are, by definition, bearers of the universal, and are themselves implicated in it. This means, first of all, that they bear the demand for the universal *here and now*: in the present moment (which, as we have seen, is *every* moment – that is to say, it is always-already time to demand emancipation for oneself and for others) and *effectively*, in a system of civic institutions and practices of citizenship which represent nothing other than the achieved dignity of every human being. To be a citizen, it is sufficient simply to be a human *being, ohne Eigenschaften.*[8] The subjects of politics are thereby also the spokespeople of the universal, in so far as they 'represent themselves' (which obviously does not exclude any institutional procedure for delegating power, on condition that it be subject to oversight, and revocable).

We should, however, remain aware that these propositions, although they have the same effectivity as all the emancipation movements there have been and will be in history, are laden with contradictions and aporias. This is the case, in particular, with the idea of representing oneself and making oneself the spokesperson of the universal, given that speech is also a power relation, and that the unequal distribution of verbal skills cannot be corrected simply by acknowledging entitlement to citizenship. But there are other examples. We must, then, sketch out a dialectic internal to emancipation.

In his book *La Mésentente*, Jacques Rancière has analysed at some length an – in my view – genuine aporia (he calls it a 'scandal of thought') which seems to me to be one of the important aspects of this dialectic.[9] He shows that politics proper – the politics which sets egalitarian logic against police logic (and which thereby distinguishes itself from anti-politics, which does the opposite) – consists not in the formation of a universal consensus within the *demos*, but in the establishment of 'the part of no part' [*part des sans-part*] (the poor in the ancient city-state; elsewhere, workers, immigrants or women, but the expression refers to a *place* – it cannot be confined to any particular sociological condition), whose existence signals the irreducible presence of a cause [*litige*] or the impossibility of constituting the *demos* as a totality, a simple distribution or reciprocity of parts.

In my view, it may, however, ensue from the fact that there is no democratic politics without such a cause [*litige*]; that there is no democratic politics at all, since the 'have-nots' (or the propertyless, the *Eigentumslosen* – the 'de-propriated' in the most general sense of the term) can neither be the subjects *of* politics – which would presuppose, for example, that they organize themselves with a view to achieving equality, conceiving themselves as the virtual *whole* of citizen humanity – nor subjects *in* politics, which would presuppose, for example, that they force an entry into the institution, so as to make their voice heard denouncing the wrong done to them, and hence establishing a public sphere from which they are excluded, but which would not exist without them. The 'have-nots' in this radical sense cannot, then, be *either a whole or a part*; their existence, which is the condition of the possibility of politics, is at the same time the condition of its impossibility.

We may also ask, however, how this aporia develops historically. The answer is that it shifts: towards what Rancière calls provocatively, and even a touch polemically, 'the pathos of the universal victim',[10] but which no doubt forms, dialectically, the process by which autonomy becomes an effective politics of emancipation. But that politics of emancipation lies not so much in the initial statement of the *de jure* fact of non-exclusion, as in the retrospective effect contained within it – an effect achieved by way of a further negation. Autonomy becomes a politics when it turns out that a 'part' of society (and hence of humanity) is excluded – legally or not – from the universal right to politics (if only in the form of a mere opposition between 'active' and 'passive' citizens – which already says it all – or, in other words, between responsible, adult citizens and 'minors'). This part (which inevitably becomes a *party*: the party of the universal, or of the abolition of particularities and classes) presents itself, then, not just as the most active mouthpiece of the citizenry, but as that fraction which is capable of presenting its own emancipation as the *criterion* of general emancipation (or as that fraction which, in continuing in slavery and alienation, inevitably entails the unfreedom of all). This, as we know, is what has been presented successively or simultaneously in the political discourse and practice of proletarians, women, colonized and enslaved peoples of colour, sexual minorities, and so on. And these examples go to show that, in reality, the whole history of emancipation is not so much the history of the demanding of unknown rights as of the real struggle to enjoy rights which *have already been declared*. If this is indeed the way things are, the battle against the denial of citizenship[11] is indeed the vital heart of the politics of emancipation. But this is certainly not without its complications, and there is, ultimately, a profound ambivalence to it.

An ambivalence on the part of the dominated, the politically excluded, who demand their particular emancipation as condition and proof of the emancipation of all, invoking the truth of the proposition of equal liberty and, by that very act, verifying its effectiveness. For this, they need to present themselves as *the people of the people*, or alternatively – to use a terminology Marx used at one time – as the universal class: the class which is simultaneously a non-class, the class whose entire being resides in its alienation; the reverse of reciprocity (of the 'free association of all', the 'community of equals'), and hence an – itself unconditional – demand for its realization. To put it plainly, it is because the autonomy of

politics presents itself first as a negation that the politics of autonomy must present itself in turn as a negation of the negation, and
thus as an absolute. The *idealization* of politics and its subjects is the
corollary to the *ideality* which grounds them (without which it would
have no practical reality). And, inevitably, this idealization expresses
itself in namings, creations of keywords, whose power to seize the
imagination is all the greater for the fact that they initially expressed
a radical negativity, the rejection of substantive representations of
'political capacity'. *People* was one such term, as was *proletariat*
(undoubtedly the pre-eminent form assumed by 'the people of the
people' in modern history). *Woman* and *foreigner* might yet become
terms of this kind.

But this ambivalence has another aspect – on the dominant side.
For this we can take as our guide Nietzsche, with his argument that
all democratic politics expresses a 'slave morality'. The most important thing here is not the counter-revolutionary stigmatization of a
politics made by and for the masses, nor the correlative idealization
of exceptional individuals, but the proposal of an analysis and a
genealogy which lay bare the mechanics by which hegemony is
constructed and consensus engineered. I shall take the liberty of
advancing the following interpretation: domination by an established order does indeed rest, as Marx argued after Hegel, on the
ideological universalization of its principles. But, contrary to what
Marx believed, the 'dominant ideas' cannot be those of the 'dominant class'. They have to be those of the 'dominated', the ideas
which state their theoretical right to recognition and equal capacity.
More precisely, the discourse of hegemonic domination has to be
one in which it is possible to appeal *against a* de facto *discrimination
to a* de jure *equality* – not only without the principles being weakened, but in such a way that they are re-established and lastingly
prove their absolute character, since it is they which, now as ever,
constitute the recourse against failure to apply them. All protest can
then turn into legitimation since, against the injustice of the
established order, protest appeals not to something heterogeneous
to that order, but to identical principles. This would ultimately not
be possible if the universal principles did not, as Nietzsche argued,
express the rights of the dominated (this, for Nietzsche, was their

crippling defect) and embody the criterion which the emancipation of the dominated represents. This is why it is almost enough for the institution of politics to be expressed as the 'right of the excluded', and this of itself, in given conditions, provides the *possibility* of a schema sanctioning the established order or consensus. This ambivalence, like the preceding one, cannot disappear as long as politics has human emancipation and citizenship as its concept. In other words, it can never disappear. Admittedly, one can also take the view that politics is precisely a practice which confronts such ambivalences. But the question then arises whether the concept which properly applies to it is still that of autonomy.

Heteronomy of Politics: Transformation

> Human beings make their own history [*machen ihre eigene Geschichte*], but they do not make it arbitrarily in conditions chosen by themselves [*selbstgewählten*], but in conditions always-already given and inherited from the past [*unmittelbar vorgefundenen, gegebenen und überlieferten*].[12]

This quotation from *The Eighteenth Brumaire of Louis Bonaparte*, which Sartre described as the concentrated essence of the historical dialectic (and the problem it poses for the philosopher), will allow us to state right at the outset the difference between a concept of the autonomy and a concept of the heteronomy of politics (which we might also call, as will become clear later, the politics of the '*Diesseits*', or pragmatism).

Undoubtedly, Marx himself did not by any means regard the two as incompatible. One might even say that the greater part of his political thinking consisted in attempting to incorporate the two into a single scenario. Like the revolutionaries whose theorist he sought to be, he was, in large measure, a Jacobin. For him, 'democracy [was] the solution to the riddle of every constitution',[13] and the proletariat was 'the universal class', whose emancipation was the touchstone for the liberation of humanity as a whole. What interests us here first of all, however, is that Marx completely overturned the assumptions of that Jacobinism, enunciating a radical conception of the heteronomy of politics, and imposing that conception on an entire period which is still our own. For Marx, exemplarily, there is no politics (no 'making of history') except *in* (*or under*) determinate *conditions* [*Umständen, Bedingungen, Verhältnissen*], into which individuals and groups 'enter' because they are always already placed in them. Far from abolishing politics, these conditions intrinsically define it, and confer reality upon it. Drawing on the key example of Marx, some of whose well-known propositions I shall recall here, I should like to outline what, in general, characterizes such a concept.

But, as we are going to discover, the interest of such a discussion also lies in the fact that there is no single model of the heteronomy of politics or of politics-under-conditions, but several, mutually opposing models, their opposition revolving around a particular point of heresy. I am not thinking here so much of the fact that various different versions of the idea of material conditions being determinant for politics can be presented, or that opposing practical consequences can be drawn from them (which Marx had already done by overturning a certain economism which was prevalent before he wrote). Nor am I thinking, even, of the fact that, in the category of social conditions or relations, one can equally well accord priority to cultural or symbolic structures, as other currents of critical sociology have done, as to structures of production and exchange. I am thinking, rather, of the fact that *the very notion of conditions* can be transmuted without the idea of an essentially heteronomous politics disappearing. Indeed, far from it. The themes elaborated by Foucault, from 'disciplinary society' to the general idea of a 'microphysics of power' and the study of 'governmentality', are exemplary in this connection. And, of course, if the way we conceive its constitutive conditions changes, then the mode of being of politics itself is transformed. The difference is properly ontological; it concerns individuality (whereas the way both differed from a concept of autonomy was, first and foremost, logical and ethical – a difference between idealism and realism or materialism).[14]

I am going to attempt, then, in a few paragraphs where several pages would really be required, to characterize not the outer envelope shared by these two conceptions, but the point at which they diverge, because it is this which is characteristic. Let us start with Marx, and begin by establishing two initial premisses, which are in fact closely linked. The truth of politics, for Marx, is to be sought not in its own self-consciousness or its constituent activity, but in the relationship it maintains with conditions and objects which form its 'material', and constitute it as a material activity in itself. But that position has nothing to do with liquidating the *autonomy of the subjects* of politics (namely, the 'people'). We might even say that the opposite is true: Marx's politics, in equal measure to the politics of emancipation, pursues the aim of establishing the autonomy of its subjects, but it regards that autonomy as a product of its own movement, not as a prior assumption. Its perspective is one of a *becoming-necessary of liberty*. Whereas the proposition of equal liberty presupposes the universality of rights, always referring these back to an ever-available transcendental origin, Marxian political practice is an internal transformation of conditions, which produces as its outcome (and quite simply produces, in so far as it is put into practice – that is, produces 'in struggle') the need for freedom and the autonomy of the people (designated as the proletariat).

We must note right away that, according to Marx, the conditions of politics are characterized as a 'base' or an 'economic structure' of history. Clearly, without this determination, we should no longer be within Marxism properly so-called, but we have to distinguish between a general and a particular aspect of that theory. It is a particular matter that Marx, actively 'reflecting' the historical process he is witnessing, and acknowledging his own involvement in the struggle developing within that process, chooses to universalize the economic base of history and, as a consequence, the anthropology which presents man as first and foremost a labouring being [*un être de travail*]. The economy understood in this sense is, pre-eminently, *the other of politics*, its absolute exterior imposing insuperable structural conditions upon it. In order to think the reality of politics, it is necessary, then, to short-circuit politics and its other (by a twofold critique: of the autonomization of politics and the fetishization of the economy). It is necessary to show that, as revolutionary politics, this reality is nothing other than the development of the contradictions of the economy.[15] To transgress the limits of the recognized – and artificially *separated* – political sphere, which are only ever the limits of the established order, politics has to get back to the 'non-political' conditions of that institution (conditions which are, ultimately, *eminently* political). It has, in other words, to get back to the economic contradictions, and gain a purchase on these from the inside.

It is this figure which is generalizable, and has, in fact, been generalized, just as – taking Marxism as a model, and linking up with new social movements (often, tactically, against Marx) – the relationship between politics and the transformation of historical 'conditions' or 'structures' different from, but no less determinant than, the economy, and no less external to the institution of the political sphere, has been theorized: in particular, those of the family or patriarchy – in other words, relations of gender domination – and those of 'symbolic capital', or intellectual and cultural relations of domination. Retrospectively, the Marxian short circuit thus appears as the prototype for a more general schema: the pattern of referring back to the material conditions of politics, which is in turn required for the internal political transformation of those conditions.[16]

Let us enunciate, then, what we may take to be Marx's theorems. The first of these states that the conditions are in reality *social relations*, or – as Althusser put it more precisely – natural-social relations. This means that they consist in the objective *ensemble* – regularly reproduced at the cost of its very contradictions – of transindividual practices (such as production, consumption, exchange, law, culture or ideological practices), and not in an accumulation of inert 'things' nor, conversely, in a transcendent curse of the human condition. As a consequence, politics is itself a determinate practice, not the utopia of an efficient administration of things, nor the eschatological hope of converting humanity to the paths of justice.

The second theorem states, as we have seen, that social relations are economic relations. But economic relations are themselves social relations. This is a new equation, the exposition of which forms the heart of the Marxian critique. I shall refer here only to the following aspect: every analysis of the social conditions of politics must bring out both the structuring causality those conditions exert and the *society-effect* (Althusser) they produce. In Marx's case, this causal structure is identified with the 'process of production and reproduction of capital' and its specific dynamic. The private ownership of the means of production is a function of this process, which is integrally related to a certain organization of communities in which, precisely, capital exerts its domination, Marx's great ambition being to show that the same elementary structure – that of the process of the exploitation of waged labour-power – constitutes the 'basis' both for a form of 'economic community' (in this case, the market or community of producer-exchangers) and for a form of state (or sovereignty and dependence, and hence a 'political community') and, consequently, for the interdependence or correlation which is sustained between them throughout history.[17]

Political practice has, then, as a condition – and this is the third theorem – the fact that *social relations (conditions) have a history*, the meaning of which is explained precisely by the dynamics of the economic process. This does not mean that the results of political practice are predetermined. Far from it. But it does mean that political practice intervenes from the inside (on the basis of its own forces, described as 'productive forces' and as 'social consciousness') into the course of a change which has always-already begun. *The capitalist structure of society cannot but change*, by virtue of its own constraints. Politics is not the mere changing of conditions, as though it were possible to isolate them and abstract from them so as to obtain a purchase on them, but it is change within change, or the *differentiation of change*, which means that the meaning of history is established only in the present.[18]

Nothing, then, is more absurd – widely held as the idea may be – than to believe such a politics to be 'subjectless' (it is history which is without a subject). I shall argue, rather, that every concept of politics implies a concept of the subject, which is specific in each case. But we have to see where the difficulties lie with a concept of the subject associated with the heteronomy of politics. In the case of Marx – we know that on this point he is the direct heir of Hegel

– the conception of the political subject relates immediately to the idea of *contradiction*. Subjectivation is the collective individualization which occurs at the point where change changes, where 'things begin to change differently' – that is to say, wherever the *tendency* immanent in the system of historical conditions finds itself affected from within by the action of an equally immanent *counter-tendency*.

It would clearly make little sense to ask which comes first, the formation of the objective counter-tendency or the movement of subjectivation, the historical activity of the subjects who, all together, form the political subject, since the two are in reality one and the same. On the other hand, it is relevant to observe the knock-on effect of this relation. Marx showed very clearly how the power of Capital (its ever-increasing productivity and apparently limitless destructiveness) feeds only on the magnitude of the resistance to which it itself gives rise.[19] The process of ongoing contradiction, in which tendency and counter-tendency do battle or negate each other, is an endless spiral. From the standpoint of politics, this also means that it is continually passing through phases of subjectivation and desubjectivation. It means that the class struggle is a formation of powers and countervailing powers, or an investment of the existing powers and countervailing powers by antagonistic forces. In short, it is a process of winning and recovering the positions of power occupied by the opposing class.

But the substance of the dialectic of contradictory tendencies is not the winning of power (without which we would very soon come back to a schema of the autonomization of politics, simply enhanced, in a merely formal way, by a reference to the class struggle). It is *the dissociation of the* antagonistic *modes of socialization* which are involved in capitalist accumulation, in which those modes develop *against* each other: on the one side, what Marx called the 'real subsumption' of individuals and their labour-power under the domination of the capitalist relation ('self-valorizing value'); on the other, what he called the free association of producers. The basic feature of this relation is precisely that it is a dissociation – that is to say, that the opposing terms are seen not as entities external to one another, to which individuals have to belong unambiguously, but as incompatible modes of existence which can, in very large measure, affect the same individuals or enjoin them to choose against their will [*contre eux-mêmes*]. So we come back here to the connection between the heteronomy of politics and the autonomization of the people.

In practice, then, we find a whole phenomenology of social existence, which provides the field, the stakes and the very substance of politics. The general form of the class struggle is not really adequate to cover this – unless we include all the modalities of existence to which the terms *individuality* and *mass* (alongside the term *class* itself) refer. Ultimately, politics as theorized by Marx is a journey of subjectivation which binds together these different modalities of practice, by illustrating the variability of the effects of a set of structural conditions. And it is here that we should look for the most interesting theorizations of politics to be found within the Marxian lineage.

Moving on now as swiftly as possible, I shall leave aside, as promised, any comparison between the Marxist conception and other conceptions of politics based on a reference to the internal contradictoriness of a structure of pre-given [*vorgefundenen*] conditions. I shall, rather, attempt the most paradoxical, but also the most instructive of confrontations – with certain of Foucault's theorizations. In a piece written in 1982 for his American audience, he declares:

> This does not deny the importance of institutions in the establishment of power relations. Instead I wish to suggest that one must analyze institutions from the standpoint of power relations, rather than vice versa, and that the fundamental point of anchorage of the relationships, even if they are embodied and crystallized in an institution, is to be found outside the institution. . . . What therefore would be proper to a relationship of power is that it be a mode of action upon actions.* That is to say, power relations are rooted deep in the social nexus, not reconstituted 'above' society as a supplementary structure whose radical effacement one could perhaps dream of. In any case, to live in society is to live in such a way that action upon other actions is possible – and in fact ongoing. A society without power relations can only be an abstraction. Which, be it said in

passing, makes all the more politically necessary the analysis of power relations in a given society, their historical formation, the source of their strength or fragility, the conditions which are necessary to transform some or to abolish others. For to say that there cannot be a society without power relations is not to say either that those which are established are necessary, or, in any case, that power constitutes a fatality at the heart of societies, such that it cannot be undermined. Instead I would say that the analysis, elaboration, and bringing into question of power relations and the 'agonism' between power relations and the intransitivity of freedom is a permanent political task inherent in all social existence.[20]

As will become clear, this text accords a central place to the vocabulary of 'conditions' and 'transformation'. But it does so by effecting a kind of reversal of Marxian ontology, regarding both the representation of relations and the relationship between practice, necessity and contingency.

Particularly interesting in this theorization, as deployed in the concrete analyses which run from *Discipline and Punish* to the Collège de France lectures on 'bio-power' and 'bio-politics',[21] is the fact that the distance between conditions and transformation is reduced to a minimum: indeed, the two become contemporaneous (in a *present* which is at once ontological, ethical and political, the analysis of which is the very aim of that critical thought which Foucault attempted, at the same moment, to redefine combining the teachings of Nietzsche and Kant). However, the fact that the practical distance disappears – that is to say, that the conditions of existence which are to be transformed are woven from the same cloth as the practice of transformation itself; that they are of the order of an 'action upon an action', and form part of an infinite network of 'asymmetrical relations' between various powers, between dominations and resistances – in no way signifies that the conceptual difference is without object.

This is why Foucault continues to talk more than ever about history and society as horizons of politics, even as – above all as – he sets about divesting institutions, large entities and the big battalions (states, classes, parties . . .) of their monopoly, to bring politics at every moment within the reach of individuals or coalitions of individuals. Between the point of view of society and that of individuals, there is total reciprocity. Society is the complex of actions which condition or transform each other. And, in reality, no action has ever succeeded in transforming another – whether it be in production, education, punishment, discipline or political liberation or constraint – other than by creating new conditions in which it can be carried out, just as no action can condition another other than by transforming it, or transforming the freedom of its bearer, as Foucault puts it. But individuals are always the singularities of this complex (or, more precisely, the *bodies* associated with all these singularities), as Deleuze rightly pointed out in his commentary on Foucault's politics.[22] What then becomes absolutely objectless is the idea of a dialectics of 'mediations' by which to conceive, following the thread of historical time, the junction between the conditions and the transformative practice, with its 'critical' encounters between objective and subjective conditions, class conflicts and mass movements, forces and consciousnesses, and so forth. For historical conflict is always-already inherent in power relations, and is always active in their institutionalization – or at least, it should be – *ideally*.

In spite of impressions to which his methodological individualism may give rise, the way Foucault constitutes politics has, then, nothing to do with reconstituting the autonomy of politics. The power relation is indeed *constituent*, whereas the more or less stabilized social forms, the norms of behaviour, are *constituted*. But the power relation is never conceived as a will or a clash of wills, conscious or unconscious. This relates in particular to the way Foucault deploys the reference to the body as ultimate referent of individuality. And, consequently, it relates to the way power relations and subjection are interpreted not in terms of mastery and servitude (of the imposition of a – just or unjust – law), but as material and spiritual technologies which 'train' bodies and dispose them to certain actions, and may reinforce or neutralize one another.

Political action must, then, as we know, be thought in terms of strategies. What is the meaning of this word, which Foucault is careful not to employ in the singular? We might say it is a general –

or generalizable – schema for the anticipation and control of the reactions of adverse individuality; or, better, a schema for the transformation of the bodily dispositions of individuals in such a way that their reactions become predictable and controllable. Such a schema can be implemented by institutions, by groups and, in the last analysis, by individuals. It can be incorporated both into a vast social structure over the very long term and into a transient, local configuration, but the principle of its effectiveness is always 'micro-political', since it lies in the way the technologies of power are applied 'right down to the finest mesh of society'.[23]

Given the foregoing summary, one might have the impression that, for Foucault, politics has passed back, if not within the ambit of the dominant, at least within that of the powerful (of those 'in power' [les gouvernants]). He himself felt the need to deny this charge, which, in a sense, was unnecessary (the imputation was the product of a misreading), but this touches, none the less, on a difficulty with which I would like to close this examination of his work. The crucial notion here is that of *resistance*. The fact that all power presupposes a resistance, and hence is based on uncertainty regarding the point at which its limits lie, does not produce any clear prescription for the form which may be assumed by the 'liberation of liberty' when the power relation is also a relation of domination. The question posed here does not merely have a pragmatic dimension; it is, fundamentally, metaphysical. Just as there was, in Marx, a problematic of the *becoming-necessary of liberty* (in the tradition of Spinoza and Hegel), so we should see in Foucault's work here (in a manner different from the 'outside' or 'foldings' of the theoretical analyses Deleuze writes of) a production of contingency, which I shall venture to term a *becoming-contingent of resistances*. But is this not the point Foucault hesitated over, while at the same time it opened up several possible directions to him, between which his politics (if not his ethics) found itself torn?

It might seem that the analytic of power relations in Foucault's work runs up against a limit constituted by the question of their dissymmetry – or, more precisely, a dissymmetry which is not 'reversible' and which might be said to be absolute. There is, first of all, the problem of the *extreme situations* in which the technologies of power as individualization of subjects (taken jointly and severally as targets for governmentality) give way not merely to a general antagonism but to naked force, exercised in the register of destruction, and of death for its own sake. Only life can be 'governed'; only a living being can be disciplined in such a way as to become productive. The question which arises here is that of practices of extermination in their various forms, some of which are, more than ever, contemporary. But there is also, in general, the question of deep-rooted structures of domination:

> The analyses I have been trying to make have to do essentially with power relations. I understand by that something different from states of domination. . . . When an individual or a social group manages to put a block on a field of power relations, to render them fixed and immobile and prevent any reversibility of movement . . . we are facing what can be called a state of domination. It is certain that in such a state the practice of liberty does not exist or exists only unilaterally or is extremely confined and limited. I agree with you that liberation is sometimes the political or historical condition for a practice of liberty. . . . Liberation opens up new power relations, which have to be controlled by practices of liberty.[24]

> In power relations, there is necessarily the possibility of resistance, for if there were no possibility of resistance – of violent resistance, of escape, of ruse, of strategies that reverse the situation – there would be no relations of power. . . . [I]f there are relations of power throughout every social field, it is because there is freedom everywhere. Now, there are effectively states of domination. In many cases power relations are fixed in such a way that they are perpetually asymmetrical and the margin of liberty is extremely limited. . . . In these cases of domination – economic, social, institutional or sexual – the problem is in fact to find out where resistance is going to organize.[25]

We can see that Foucault is compelled here to stretch out the time of the strategic present, in which the asymmetry of power relations previously always led to the immediate possibility of an overturning or a displacement: structures have appeared (of the order of constraint, the law and the norm) from which subjects are in some way separated – structures which 'instil' power relations into the very intimacy of bodies in a manner over which subjects have no control. To the problem posed by these structures, Foucault can respond only by the classical recourse to 'social movements', his only original point being the assertion that the range of social movements is coextensive with the range of all relations of domination which may form in society, and that they therefore have no pre-established form of organization.

However, the indication that practices of liberty are not so much the precondition for liberation as a necessity emerging after the event leads us in another direction. This is the direction which, in the end, comes increasingly to monopolize Foucault's attention: the analysis of 'technologies of the Self'. It is still beset by difficulty, as the idea of resistance now raises the question of how individuals' relationships to their own selves develop, and how such a relationship can itself change sign or regime. There is a danger, then, that we shall be caught up in an infinite regress. Foucault wants to turn this ultimate difficulty into a virtue: that is to say, he wants to analyse not the power, but the 'self' of the individual, and its mode of production or creation (the 'aesthetics' of the self). This move is Stoic in inspiration, except that it is not so much a question of tracing a dividing line between what depends on us and what does not as of showing how, in a way, the modality of what does not depend on us (for example, domination) is still determined by what does. In this sense, the study of the techniques of the self is not so much an evasion of the question posed by massive structures of domination as the search for a more originary level of determination and, as a result, for a point of construction – or deconstruction – for politics.

I shall argue here that this move is, in the last analysis, not merely incomplete, and hence still open, but philosophically aporetic. The aporia bears precisely on the notions of 'self' or individuality. It is clear that Foucault has not in any sense elaborated these critically (Deleuze attempted to do it for him); he has just taken them, empirically and eclectically, as he found them. What is most interesting here, however, is to set Foucault's aporia alongside that of Marx. As we might expect, they relate to opposite terms, but they are both inherent in the central idea of *transformation*. By making 'social relations of production' – namely capital and its indefinite process of expansion – both the external, *vorgefundenen* conditions of political practice and the element in which its internal negativity or its process of revolutionary division develops, Marx presented as the ultimate horizon of any effective transformation (encompassing the *totality of conditions*) what he himself called from the outset the transformation of the world [*Veränderung der Welt*], which assumes the emergence (elsewhere than in the imagination) of a world-politics and a subject of politics who is him- or herself 'global' [*mondial*]. Now, this notion is clearly dialectical – not in this case in the sense of the historical development of contradictions, but in the sense of the Kantian critique of the antinomies of reason (if only of practical reason). It simply engages us in an infinite regress, the terms of which have become perfectly visible since the world has effectively become 'globalized'.[26]

Conversely, Foucault, though forearming himself against the classical forms of the paralogism of personality by shifting the question of the 'self' and its constitution from the terrain of consciousness and substance to that of corporeity (the great strength of Foucault is his explaining that the production of interiority is located entirely in the 'outside [*le dehors*]', the constitution of the subject in objectivity), and hence of *ascesis*, has probably still not escaped reproducing that paralogism in a new form in so far as he makes the 'work of self upon self' both the passive (the historicity of modes of subjectivation) and the active side of the process (the production, not to say the shaping, of his or her style of life and thought) of that production. This 'work of self on self' generates, then, both the normal form of a culture and the deliberately run risk of becoming different from what one was. This 'double-bind' situation is no less dialectical (in the Kantian sense) than the preceding one. Hence the latent oscillation between a (periodically denied) fatalism and a *de facto* voluntarism, to which the Nietz-schean reference does not really provide a corrective.

It would be wrong to conclude from all this that the idea of politics as transformation falls down in the end. Just as the aporias of emancipation constantly provide new impetus for the reformulation – and the re-demanding – of emancipation, so the fact that a radical formulation of the idea of transformation runs up either against the aporia of the 'transformation of the world' or against that of the 'production of oneself', which together delimit the field of problems it poses (and which it imposes on politics), does not disqualify it. It is, rather, a wellspring of permanent invention. For such a conception really to be confronted with the impossible, we have to pass on to another stage [*une autre scène*].

The Heteronomy of Heteronomy: The Problem of Civility

In an interview conducted in 1983, Foucault spoke of 'problems which come at politics from an unexpected quarter.'[27] These problems are, in a sense, the most immediate ones. The ones I want to talk about now come at politics through violence (and cruelty), through identity (and identity politics) and through the 'perverse effects' of rationality and universality. We can start out from two texts which are very distinct in inspiration. The first is by the psychoanalyst Fethi Benslama, attempting to reflect on 'the crossing of a new limit in human destructiveness' which the current attempts at 'ethnic cleansing' evoke:

The foreigner in question does not establish or distinguish, cannot be either dialecticized or overcome, offers a glimpse of neither sanctity nor healing, is not absolute and does not abolutize. . . . His foreignness is not due to the fact that he is other or comes from elsewhere. He is, rather, someone (or a group or set of individuals) very close, very familiar, closely intermingling with oneself as an inextricable part of oneself. All the ravages of identity problems arise precisely out of this condition in which foreignness has emerged from the substance of communal identity in the greatest possible intermingling of images, affects, languages and references. So, when the imperious need spreads to reappropriate the '*propre*'[28] – which is the watchword of all cleansings – the purifying, avenging rage is set not on vanquishing the enemy or driving him out, but on mutilating and exterminating him, as though it were a question of rooting out the foreign body and extirpating from the body the foreigner attaching to the representation of one's own body. . . . It is a breach within the *We* which can no longer either be made good or expelled. . . . This is the disorder of the dis-identification of a self unrepresentable to oneself, living in fear of a foreignness emanating from the depths of its being. The effects of such a situation can be contained politically, and only the political sphere is capable of containing them. But if the political institution failed or collapsed . . . we would then see a return of the annihilation anxiety and the unleashing of the purifying forces which proceed by mutilation and self-mutilation, so intimately are self and other enmeshed.[29]

The second, older, text is by Deleuze and Guattari:

Why are there so many becomings of man, but no becoming-man? First because man is a majoritarian *par excellence*, whereas becomings are minoritarian; all becoming is a becoming-minoritarian. When we say majority, we are referring not to a greater relative quantity but to the determination of a state or standard in relation to which larger quantities, as well as the smallest, can be said to be minoritarian: white-man, adult-male, etc. Majority implies a state of domination, not the reverse. . . . It is perhaps the special situation of women in relation to the man-standard that accounts for the fact that becomings, being minoritarian, always pass through a becoming-woman. It is important not to confuse 'minoritarian', as a becoming or process, with a 'minority' as an aggregate or a state. Jews, Gypsies, etc., may constitute minorities under certain conditions, but that in itself does not make them becomings. One reterritorializes, or allows oneself to be reterritorialized, on a minority as a state; but in a becoming, one is deterritorialized. Even blacks, as the Black Panthers said, must become-black. Even women must become-women. Even Jews must become-Jewish. . . . But if this is the case, then becoming-Jewish necessarily affects the non-Jew as much as the Jew. Becoming-woman necessarily affects men as much as women. In a way, the subject in a becoming is always 'man', but only when he enters a becoming-minoritarian that rends him from his major identity. . . . This is the opposite of macropolitics, and even of history, in which it is a question of knowing how to win or obtain a majority. As Faulkner said, to avoid ending up a fascist there was no other choice than to become-black.[30]

In many ways, I ought to develop the third concept I advance here as a discussion between (and with) Benslama and Deleuze/Guattari, evaluating what unites and what divides them. But I do not have room for this. I shall begin, rather, by attempting to specify the terms of the enigma constituted by the fusion of the problem of violence and the problem of identity, from the point when one decides not to accept the simple self-evidence of their relationship. This unity, which is neither necessary (as though the conjunction of violence and identity were part of the essence of these concepts) nor contingent (as though it occurred by chance), takes us back to what I shall term abstractly, in reference to what has preceded, a heteronomy of the heteronomy of politics. I shall then go on to test out the concept of *civility* as a way of characterizing the politics which takes as its 'object' the very violence of identities.

Let us first consider violence in its extreme forms – what I have elsewhere termed *cruelty*, emphasizing its permanent oscillation between ultra-naturalist, ultra-objective and ultra-subjective forms, paroxysms of intentionality (including when that intentionality is turned upon itself and is, therefore, 'suicidal' as well as 'lethal').[31] Bertrand Ogilvie has recently examined this question of the *new*, specifically modern patterns of violence, in which the frontier between the natural and the social tends to become blurred, and he has brought them together under the heading of a terrible term borrowed from Latin American Spanish: the 'making of disposable man [*poblacion chatarra*]'.[32] He takes as his examples all those forms of 'indirect and delegated extermination' which consist in 'abandoning' the excess populations on the world market 'to their fate' (a fate made up of 'natural' catastrophes, pandemics, reciprocal genocides or, more ordinarily, of a periodic cleansing – at the murky frontiers where criminality conjoins with the action to police it – such as the murder of children in the Brazilian *favelas*). He does, however, also point out that there are, at the margins, a number of operations providing humanitarian cover for all this. And there are also a number of enterprises seeking to make money out of exclusion by exploiting human material (trade in organs, trafficking of children, etc.). With this 'fantastic pressure for a-subjectivity' we are clearly as far as we can be from any power relation of the kind Foucault proposed for theorization. We are also at a place where any claim to a right to political action has become risible: not because the universality of the human condition would not be at issue, or would merely be the expression of a domineering rationality, but because there is practically no possibility for the victims to see themselves and present themselves *in person* as political subjects, capable of emancipating humanity by emancipating themselves. Might this be because certain historical *conditions* are not (or not yet) realized? And what can we say, generally, about the relationship between such practices of elimination and the idea of structural violence?

I shall say that, ultimately, it is not the same thing or, more exactly, that these practices shatter the representation of the idea. By structural violence, we generally understand an oppression inherent in social relations which (by all means, from the most ostentatious to the most invisible, from the most economical to the most costly in human lives, from the most everyday to the most exceptional) breaks down that resistance which is incompatible with the reproduction of a system. In that sense, it is an integral part of the life of the system, or accompanies it like a shadow. The functionality which characterizes it may, in absolute terms, be totally irrational; it may well show itself only after the event, as an 'invisible hand'. Yet it is no less necessary to see it as such if we are to be able to identify the interests, power positions and forms of social domination to which it corresponds (slavery, patriarchy or capital), and pose the problem of overturning them. However, with the totally non-functional elimination of millions of disposable people – an elimination which, none the less, figures in precise terms in the planning schedules of the world-economy (and which might express a certain inability to exploit which is 'arresting' the current development of capital: in other words, an inability to cope with the financial, security-related, ideological and, in the last analysis, political costs of a truly globalized accumulation process) – we have in fact passed beyond this limit of structural violence. In other words, we have entered a world of the banality of objective cruelty which goes beyond any mere reproduction of structures.[33]

However, while we cannot posit an unambiguous causal relation here, such ultra-objective forms of violence find themselves existing alongside – or superimposed locally or temporally upon – other forms of an opposite kind. And we are talking not just about the spread of 'aimless violence' (Ogilvie), the kind generally classified as petty offending behaviour, which is not aimed at achieving any kind of transformation, and merely expresses hopeless revolt and a hatred of a social order presented as entirely 'natural'. Above all, what we are concerned with here is what we are compelled to call ultra-subjective forms of violence. In particular, those inversions of the will to power into a will to 'de-corporation', to forced disaffiliation from the other and from oneself – not just from belonging to the community and the political unit, but from the human condition, which Benslama describes in relation to ethnic cleansing in Bosnia (the massacre of pupils by their own teachers, collective rapes designed to produce enemy babies in the wombs of the women of the opposing community, etc., at the same time as all the monuments of multicultural history are razed to the ground) – these forms of violence which lead him to ask if it might not be necessary to theorize not just 'beyond the pleasure principle', but 'beyond the death drive'!

Here we are not in the realm of ordinary forms of fascism (which it is time to acknowledge as a constant factor in the construction and destruction of states and the clash between 'social systems' in the twentieth century), but in that of the multiplication – possible anywhere, within any culture – of that *idealization of hatred*[34] which was, somewhat hastily after Nazism, declared unique and beyond all possibility of repetition. I call it ultra-subjective violence because such actions are undoubtedly intentional and have a determinate goal. They also have a face – that of persecutors who are all too human, cruel and cowardly, cunning and stupid – but the will which gives rise to them can only be described, ultimately, as the expression of a 'thing' (to use Freud's term, picked up on by Lacan) of which the subject is the mere instrument: of that identity which is (which he 'believes' to be) in him, an identity totally exclusive of any other, one which imperiously commands its self-realization through the elimination of any trace of otherness in the 'we' and in the 'self'. An identity disposed as a consequence to 'prefer' one's own death to what seems to it to be the lethal danger of a mixing or a de-propriation.

In each of these extreme forms or figures, we have to see the mark of an irreducible fact, which is not simply the 'evil' of violence but its non-convertibility (or non-dialecticity). More precisely, the proof that a certain violence can neither be repressed or kept down (which is, broadly, the objective of theorizations of the political as justice, *logos*, social bond), nor converted politically into a means of 'making history': by combining individual acts of violence into collective violence and using such violence, deliberately or otherwise, as a means of taking power and consolidating it institutionally by associating it with ideological hegemonies, or as a means of emancipation and transformation. Such violence is the stuff of both politics and history; it tends to become (or become again) a permanent *condition* of the unfolding of politics and history (at least in the sense that there is no longer any question of their leaving violence behind), yet it marks the limit of reciprocal actions: of the passage of politics into the field of historicity, and of historical conditions into the scope of politics. This is why I propose to see here, above and beyond the heteronomy of politics, a heteronomy of heteronomy which throws into question the idea of the constitution of politics either as transformation or emancipation. Yet there *still* has to be (logically or ethically) a politics involved in the condition of subjects collectively confronted with the limits of their own power. Or at least, we have to raise the question of such a thing.

In doing this, we should no doubt review two of the terms we have just employed: 'extreme' forms and 'limits'. What extremes do we mean? And where are we to set limits? We shall have to accept the idea that these limits cannot be assigned – or that, at any rate, they are not fixed – because the ultra-objectivity of violence is always written, at least latently, into the naturalization of the relations of domination (or even in what, combining Marx's and Foucault's terminologies, we might call the naturalization of asymmetrical relations of power); and the ultra-subjectivity of violence is written into any subjection of individuals to the rule of a spiritual authority which is sufficiently ferocious and incomprehensible to demand 'more than death'. In reality, then, these limits are successive thresholds, belonging to both private and public spheres – limits transgressed institutionally or in the course of individual existences, and in some cases interconnected. We can see from this (without this actually solving the enigma of these limits) that their history is never separable from the way identities themselves are fixed or transformed. Rather than embark on a long discussion of this point here, I shall advance three theses, referring the reader elsewhere for a more complete justification of the argument.[35]

The first thesis is that all identity is fundamentally transindividual. This means that it is neither (purely) individual nor (purely) collective. What is known as the 'self' can (in the best of cases) be experienced as absolutely singular, as a personal content of existence irreducible to any model or role, either elective or imposed. It is none the less constructed (from before birth) by a system of real and symbolic social relations. Conversely, a collective identity – in other words, the constitution of a relation of belonging or a 'we' (and an 'us': we belong to the community – for example, the fatherland, at whose disposal we stand, or the family, which can require our support – and they belong to 'us', which means that we must not be deprived of them) – is only ever the constitution of a bond which is, in reality, validated among individual imaginations. But this imaginary register is as indispensable to the life of individuals as the air they breathe. That is why, though 'nations are not made by nature' (Spinoza), no individual can take up a place (except, precisely, in imagination) in the 'original situation' which precedes nations (or their equivalent).

This brings us to a second thesis. Rather than identities, we should speak of identifications and processes of identification, for no identity is either given or acquired once and for all (it can be *fixed*, but that is not the same thing). Identity is the product of an invariably uneven, unfinished process, of hazardous constructions requiring greater or lesser symbolic guarantees. Identification is received from others, and continues always to depend on them. In establishing the many circles of identity which are superimposed upon each other in this way, reinforcing or combating one another, material conditions naturally have their full impact, translating themselves into possibilities – and impossibilities – of communication, and of access to 'common goods' of all kinds. But the ultimate condition is constituted by the existence of institutions, on which the possibility of symbolizing roles (one's own and other people's) and the formation or breaking of bonds depends. This applies whether these institutions are very old or very recent, and whether they are official and dominant (such as those Althusser referred to as 'ideological state apparatuses') or oppositional and 'anti-system'.

This gives rise to our third thesis: every identity is *ambiguous*. We may understand this from the subject's point of view: no individual (except in *borderline*-situations – a point to which I shall return), whatever he says or believes, has a single identity, which would mean also a single sense of belonging. Every individual combines several identities, which are unevenly significant, unevenly conflicted. However, it is even more interesting to look at this from the standpoint of identity itself, which cannot be univocal. An identity of whatever kind (sexual, occupational, religious, national, linguistic, aesthetic . . .) is always overdetermined. It always fulfils several functions at one and the same time (one is not a 'teacher' *only* to teach one's students, and even less is one a student *simply* to study). It is always in transit between several symbolic references (for example, current events cause us to ask once again, without any possible resolution of the question, whether Islam today is a religious, national-cultural or anti-imperialist identity). In this sense, too, identity is always *wide of the mark*; it is always in danger of mistaking itself or being mistaken. It always has to express itself successively through different commitments.

These theses enable us, I think, at least to pose the question of how violence and identities connect (what happens when conflicts of identity become destructive or self-destructive? What happens when current violence, whether structural or transient in origin, crystallizes around identity-claims and impositions of identity?).

Coming at this from the question of identity, we might suggest that *two extreme situations are equally impossible.* They are impossible in the sense that they are unliveable, that they correspond to a zero degree of autonomy to the point where a normal existence or normal communication are destroyed. But not in the sense that these situations would never be required, engendered or imposed by historical conditions and institutions. This is perhaps why there is inconvertible violence. One of these situations is that in which individuality might be reduced to a 'massive', 'exclusive', *single, unambiguous identity* (being only a woman, or a man, or a child – in other words, a sexual object; being only a teacher or a worker, a company boss, a president, an activist, a good pupil or faithful believer, totally identified with one's role: that is to say, immediately absorbing any other role or encounter into one's function or calling, one's *Beruf*; being only a Frenchman, a Jew, a Breton or a Serb . . .). The other situation is that which – in keeping with a certain 'postmodern' utopia, but also with a certain demand for elasticity engendered by the spread of market relations – would allow identity to *float freely* between all roles, between casual, pleasurable (or advantageous) identifications: being *absolutely one* or being *no one.* And we can perhaps hypothesize that certain situations of violence with which we are faced occur not simply when individuals or groups are carried towards one of these extremes, but when these respective impossibilities meet, when individuals or groups seek a way out in a violent oscillation from one pole to the other.

We must, then, suppose that the role of institutions is precisely to reduce – without suppressing– the multiplicity, complexity and conflictuality of identifications and senses of belonging, if need be by applying a preventive violence or a 'symbolic' and material – corporeal – organized counter-violence. This is why there is no society (no viable or liveable society) without institutions and counter-institutions (with the oppressions they legitimate and the revolts they induce). But institutions are not a politics. At most they can be the instruments or the products of a politics.

I shall call a politics which regulates the conflict of identifications between the impossible (and yet, in a sense, very real) limits of a total and a floating identification, 'civility'. Civility in this sense is certainly

not a politics which suppresses all violence; but it excludes extremes
of violence, so as to *create a* (public, private) *space* for politics
(emancipation, transformation), and enable violence itself to be
historicized. What interests me, here, is not to codify that civility, but
to attempt, in conclusion, to outline some of its problems.[36]

The first major problem is to determine whether any politics – as
civility – is necessarily made 'from the top down' or, in other words,
by the action and authority of a 'master' (albeit only an inner
master),[37] or whether it can also be made 'from below' by the effort
of individuals and collectives employing their own force. It might
seem that the question is settled in advance, because political
philosophy (and also the religious and sociological traditions) have
always taught that the multitude is intrinsically violent, and have
always connected the need for education with the institution of a
judicial system and a social order which, even if it had no other
hierarchy, assumed that there was a government and forms of
power – assumed, let us say, that there was hegemony. It is also as a
creator of civility that a government can appear legitimate (beginning with the power of law). But it is so as to appear as the only
conceivable creator of civility that the established power elaborates
a theory of the passions of the multitude as an inexhaustible,
threatening reservoir of incivility.

However, the form in which it is most interesting to discuss the
question is that which attempts, conversely, to reconcile the idea of
civility with that of an autonomy of the multitude – that is to say,
with democratic forms. I might even be tempted to argue that
civility *becomes a politics*, in the strong sense of the term – distinct
from a civic education or discipline, or even a socialization – every
time in history it presents itself as the development of – or comple-
ment to – the democratic principle. And, from this point of view,
the most complex philosophical elaboration is that proposed by
Hegel (particularly in the *Philosophy of Right*). In order to progress a
little at this point, I shall borrow a number of general themes from
him.

Hegel's idea of civility is the counterpart to his dialectical conviction that, in history, violence is convertible ('the real is rational'),
provided it is preventively processed [*traitée*] by a state which is,

itself, a *Rechtsstaat* – that is to say, a state which constitutes itself with the intention of liberating individuals. And the kernel of this is the exposition of a process of reciprocal mediation between the particular and the universal enabling the individual to *belong* to multiple (family, regional, religious, occupational, political . . .) 'communities', and hence to maintain *concrete* identities – and the 'honour' of those identities – while acquiring (by law, education, public functions and social citizenship) a universal – or, better, universalizing – *abstract* identity which superimposes itself upon the preceding ones, and becomes their condition of possibility. More precisely, Hegel's idea is that primary identities and senses of belonging have to be virtually destroyed in order to be not purely and simply eliminated, but reconstructed as particular expressions and mediations of collective political identity, or a belonging to the state. Clearly, this assumes a differential treatment of primary identities, a selection from among them, a ranking of their importance in terms of the interests of the state and hence of the recognition of those identities, and in all cases a de-naturing. To use a different parlance, let us say that there is a simultaneous double movement of *disidentification* and *identification*, but this is controlled in advance by the state or the 'higher' community, so that the result is *guaranteed*, since it has been prepared well in advance by the ethical formations of civil society. This movement clearly has universalistic implications, and indeed it produces an effect of *intensive* universalization, because it takes the individual out of his 'natural' confinement within a single community (the model for which is the family) by opening up a space of free play for him in which – at times simultaneously and at others successively – he will assume several roles or personalities. All in all, it allows each subject to move from 'membership' to 'joining', which always presupposes the relative possibility of a choice, albeit a choice from within a pre-existing social framework.

We can take it as read, following Hegel, that the movement of disidentification–identification is the very heart of a concept of civility. We might also call this appropriation–disappropriation. Yet what holds us back from subscribing to Hegelianism is a triple nondialectizable contradiction at the heart of Hegel's theoretical edifice. First, Hegel is not aware, or pretends not to be aware, that the deconstruction of primary identities, even as – and particularly as – the price to be paid for a liberation, is a process which is in itself extremely violent; it is a 'disincorporation' or 'dismemberment' of the individual, and of the sense of belonging which provided him with a status of membership. He does not raise the question of the cost and subsequent effects of this freedom in terms of internal or external aggression.[38] Second, he is not aware, or pretends not to be aware, that the *universalistic* community (the state), however republican and secular it may be, must also be a *community*. In the modern age it is, in practice, a national or quasi-national community, whose subjects have *also* to imagine their common belonging, and, at a deeper level, to constitute in the imaginary register the commonly appropriated 'substance' of their political identity. Elsewhere I have proposed the term *fictive ethnicity* for this quasi-genealogical entity, formed out of family, linguistic or religious bonds, and vested in the sites and myths of historical memory, and so on. What we have here is an identification of disidentification. It is the mediation necessary for propelling barbarism outside one's borders, for attributing it to 'others', a move correlating with enjoyment of peace and civilization within one's borders. And when globalization emerges (or, rather, when it reaches a new stage), it prepares the ground (conjointly with other totalizing – traditional or reactive – identifications) for the reproduction, on an expanded scale, of the conflict over what is or is not to be integrated. Now, in the globalized space, in which borders are both hystericized and vacillating, in which the transnational machinery of communications, surveillance and credit reaches into individuals' own homes, there is no equivalent to the state and its *Sittlichkeit*, no 'civilizing heights'. The only heights, apparently, are those occupied by TV and information satellites.

This brings us to the third contradiction. In this case, we cannot point to a denial on Hegel's part, but we may argue that he was wrong about its development. In calling the system of market relations dominated by the imperative of valorizing value 'civil society' [*bürgerliche Gesellschaft*], and in assigning it the essential function of preparing the individualization of subjects by dissolving traditional ties and spreading contractual relations, Hegel was aware that the state (or politics) constructs its own universality only by incorporating into itself the destructive power (the negativity) inherent in its other, the economic process. But did he understand that this latter, far from being confined to a subordinate role in the service of the ethical universal and the political institution, was ultimately capable of breaking down any power which was not that of 'abstract labour'? Here we are at the ambiguous point in Hegel's theorization, since on the one hand he explains clearly that the autonomous movement of private property relentlessly produces a polarization between a wealth which exceeds all needs and a poverty which falls far below subsistence level, but, on the other, he presents this polarization of *Klassen*, which is destructive of the very conditions of civility, as a *marginal* phenomenon. It will fall to Marx to explain that what Hegel regarded as marginal was in reality central.[39]

The perspective can then be reversed, and we have to ask not whether the state never plays any role in the constitution of a civility, but in what conditions and within what limits it may do so. Must we not seriously doubt whether the state, *on its own*, is really an agent of civility? Marx suggested that we should when, against the socialists' projects for national popular education, he contended in the *Critique of the Gotha Programme* that the state had need of a 'rude education by the people'.[40] Looking at the history of the twentieth century, we may well take the view that this is what has happened, albeit in an entirely local and provisional way: that 'multitudes' – 'ordinary' citizens, classes, 'mass' parties – have come together to force the state to *recognize* their dignity, and to introduce norms of civility into public service or the public sphere. They have done so precisely in so far as they have used the state and its institutions (schools, the legal and political systems) to civilize themselves – that is to say, in the first instance, to represent the world to themselves as a shared space in which they have their place. Once again, we might ask, was this 'slave morality' at work? It might, rather, seem that such an initiative would never have got off the ground without the 'multitude' having a sufficient degree of autonomy, without autonomous 'practices of the self' being constantly invented by those making up that multitude.

This is why we have to turn once again to the question which led us to refer at the beginning of this section to Deleuze and Guattari's text. What is at the 'bottom' of this 'bottom–up' civility? Or, to put it another way, what is the multitude? From Deleuze's standpoint, the multitude is minorities; or rather (since he explains very clearly that minorities are state functions, 'territorial' functions), it is the processes of becoming-minoritarian which radically privilege disidentification over any identification, over any collective self-recognition in a normative model (or 'standard'). We shall not ask here whether the examples Deleuze cites (blacks, women, Jews) are tenable, or whether any example whatever is tenable (he would probably reply that this is a circle: it is not a question of *given* black or Jewish identity, but of the sign of a possibility in a certain conjuncture). We shall ask, rather, whether the same dialectization (I hold to the term) should not be applied, symmetrically, to the notion of *majority*.

Deleuze and Guattari's thinking stands entirely within a perspective of anti-fascism, and hence – even if they do not employ the term – of a politics of civility. The point is to determine at what level the transmutation of individuality must be rooted for the becoming-fascist of the masses – the emergence of a desire which 'desires its own repression' – to become impossible.[41] Yet may we not, here again, suggest that between the anti-fascism of the majority multitudes and that of the minority multitudes there prevails a kind of antinomy of practical reason? Each point of view feeds on the refutation of its opposite. For a micro-politics of desire, the organization of mass movements aiming to control the state, and hence to invest it from within, to gain its recognition or to transform it in a revolutionary way, is linked to a hegemonic project, with the constitution of a 'total', if not indeed totalitarian, ideology, and with the representation of society as a whole divided into antagonistic parts which runs the constant danger of ending in an 'idealization of hatred'. For a macro-politics of social citizenship, the 'machinic assemblages of desire', aiming to de-territorialize all formations and de-formations of groups, are always in danger of falling involuntarily, if not contingently, into step with trends working to naturalize 'social connectivity' and radical deindividualization, which are merely the obverse of the communications, consumption and control megamachine. Disincorporation is a double-edged sword. The political hypothesis of a civility 'from below' cannot, then, choose between the strategy (or language) of the becoming-majoritarian or the becoming-minoritarian of resistance, since it defines itself both as an alternative to the violence inherent in the state, and as a remedy for the state's impotence in respect of the two faces of cruelty. If this is not a theoretical choice, then it is a conjunctural question, a question of the art of politics – and perhaps simply of art, since the only means civility has at its disposal are statements, signs and roles.

Two remarks in conclusion. I have used the term *aporia* throughout with regard to each concept of politics, while attempting not to confuse this notion with that of impasse. We may reformulate this as follows: no concept of politics is complete. Each presupposes the others in the space and historical time of 'life'. No emancipation without transformation or civility; no civility without emancipation or transformation, and so on. But there is no sense trying to turn these complex presuppositions into a system, or arrange them in some invariant order. If we do that, we shall obtain only another political philosophy, a schema for the transformation of political problems into a representation of *the political.* In so far as the concepts we have discussed here concern politics, they can be articulated only on individual pathways (or, more precisely, at the meeting-point of individual pathways). Such pathways, like truth, are necessarily singular; hence no model exists for them.

Notes

This essay was first published as an article in *Les Temps Modernes*, 587, March–April–May 1996. An amended and expanded version was published in Étienne Balibar, *La Crainte des masses. Politique et philosophie avant et après Marx* (Paris: Gaililée, 1997).

    1. To distinguish it from *extensive* universalities, which seek to gather humanity – or the greater part of it – together under a single authority, belief system or form of hope, if not indeed a mere shared 'way of life'.

2. This term [*égaliberté* in French] is a contraction of 'equal liberty'. See Étienne Balibar, ' "Droits de l'homme" et "Droits du citoyen". La dialectique moderne de l'égalité et de la liberté', in *Les Frontières de la démocratie* (Paris: La Découverte, 1992), pp. 124–50/ ' "Rights of Man" and "Rights of the Citizen": The Modern Dialectic of Equality and Freedom', in Balibar, *Masses, Classes, Ideas: Studies in Politics and Philosophy before and after Marx* (London: Routledge, 1993), ch. 2, pp. 39–59. The expression comes from the Roman '*aequa libertas*', and is still current in debates over contemporary neo-contractualism.

3. Antonio Negri, *Insurgencies: Constituent Power and the Modern State*, trans. Maurizia Boscagli, (Minneapolis and London: University of Minnesota Press, 1999).

4. 'Man is born free, and is everywhere in chains', wrote Rousseau. The Declaration of 1789 stated in what we would today call performative mode: 'Men are born and remain free and equal in rights.'

5. That is to say, when it is not 'qualified' restrictively by the introduction of an *order of priority* between the two values or 'principles' it asserts (liberty in equality and equality in liberty), as is the case, for example, in Rawls (*Theory of Justice*), who takes up the classical formula (not by chance, we must suppose), only to state immediately that the former is unconditional, while the latter can only be conditional.

6. 'What is Enlightenment? Enlightenment is man's emergence from his self-incurred immaturity. Immaturity is the inability to use one's own understanding without the guidance of another. This immaturity is self-incurred if its cause is not lack of understanding, but lack of resolution and courage to use it without the guidance of another.' Kant, *Political Writings* (Cambridge: Cambridge University Press, second edition, 1991), p. 54.

7. The preamble to the Provisional Rules of the International Working Men's Association, drawn up by Marx in 1864, is entirely in keeping with this conception: 'The emancipation of the working classes must be conquered by the working classes themselves.'

8. Without qualities [Trans.].

9. Jacques Rancière, *Disagreement: Politics and Philosophy*, trans. Julie Rose, (Minneapolis: University of Minnesota Press, 1998).

10. Ibid., p. 63.

11. And through that denial the denial of humanity, for the denial of citizenship is always based on the exhibiting of some anthropological differentiation which can be set against universality in the name of the characteristics of the human species: maternal function, racial or intellectual inferiority, alleged inadmissibility or abnormality, etc.

12. In order to follow Balibar closely here, I have made my own translation of this text from Marx's *Der achtzehnte Brumaire des Louis Bonaparte*. The bracketed passages in German are included by Balibar. The expression he translates as '*arbitrairement*' is, in Marx's original, '*aus freien Stücken*'. A more familiar translation of this passage runs as follows: 'Men make their own history, but not of

their own free will; not under circumstances they themselves have chosen but under the given and inherited circumstances with which they are directly confronted'. Marx, *Surveys from Exile*, (Harmondsworth: Penguin Books in association with *New Left Review*, 1973), p. 146. [Trans.]

13. 'Critique of Hegel's Doctrine of the State', in *Early Writings* (Harmondsworth: Penguin Books in association with New Left Review, 1975), p. 87.

14. Some readers will wonder why I do not refer here to Max Weber, but my aim is not to be all-inclusive but, rather, to seek out a specific difference. Marx and Foucault are not chosen at random, but nor do they exhaust the entire question. On the 'standpoint of the *Diesseits*' shared by Marx and Weber, see Catherine Colliot-Thélène, *Max Weber et l'histoire* (Paris: PUF, 1990), pp. 35 ff.

15. On this short circuit which is characteristic of Marx, see my earlier essay 'L'idée d'une politique de classe chez Marx', *Les Temps Modernes*, 451, February 1984/'In Search of the Proletariat: The Notion of Class Politics in Marx', in *Masses, Classes, Ideas*, ch. 5, pp. 125–49.

16. The work originally published in 1970 by Pierre Bourdieu, Jean-Claude Passeron *et al.*, *Reproduction in Education, Society and Culture*, second edition (London: Sage, 1990), is very characteristic of this position. It was roundly attacked on these grounds by the *Révoltes logiques* collective in *L'empire du sociologue* (Paris: La Découverte, 1984).

17. See Marx, *Capital*, Volume III (Harmondsworth: Penguin Books in Association with New Left Review, 1991), p. 927, and my commentary in 'In Search of the Proletariat'.

18. I have presented this aspect of Marx's thought – which economistic, evolutionary Marxism quickly consigned to oblivion – in Chapter 4 of *The Philosophy of Marx*, trans. Chris Turner (London and New York: Verso, 1995), pp. 80–112.

19. This is the whole 'secret' of *relative surplus-value*, which he sets at the heart of the process of intensive accumulation or the 'real subsumption of labour'. *Capital*, Volume 1, trans. Ben Fowkes (Harmondsworth: Penguin Books in association with New Left Review, 1976), Part IV: 'The Production of Relative Surplus Value', pp. 427–639.

20. Michel Foucault, 'The Subject and Power', in Hubert L. Dreyfus and Paul Rabinow, *Michel Foucault: Beyond Structuralism and Hermeneutics* (Brighton: Harvester Press, 1982) pp. 222–3.

I have preferred not to modify this text, as it seems likely that it was written by Foucault directly in English. However, the sentence marked with an asterisk, if it had been translated from the French of Foucault's *Dits et Écrits*, would be more properly rendered as: 'It might be said, then, to be the specific feature [*le propre*] of a power relation that it is a mode of action on actions.' The phrase in the above passage 'that power constitutes a fatality at the heart of societies, such that it cannot be undermined' is, in the French, quite simply 'que . . . le pouvoir constitue au cœur des sociétés une fatalité incontournable'. [Trans.]

21. For a remarkable discussion of these lectures see Ann Laura Stoler, *Race*

and the Education of Desire: Foucault's History of Sexuality and the Colonial Order of Things (Durham, NC: Duke University Press, 1995).

22. Giles Deleuze, 'Qu'est-ce qu'un dispositif?', in Michel Foucault, philosophe (Paris: Seuil, 1989).

23. Foucault does not by any means believe that power strategies are applied automatically, an argument which would lead to transforming the theory of politics into a formal 'strategic analysis'. He is, rather, systematically concerned with the discrepancy between strategic anticipations and the methods or procedures of real government, which he terms 'usage'. This point is particularly well illustrated in his analysis of prisons (see, in particular, the 1984 interview 'Qu'appelle-t-on punir?', reprinted in Michel Foucault, Dits et Écrits, IV, pp. 636 ff.)

24. 'The Ethic of Care for the Self as a Practice of Freedom: An Interview with Michel Foucault on January 20, 1984, conducted by Raul Fornet-Betancourt, Helmut Becker, Alfredo Gomez-Müller', Philosophy and Social Criticism, XII, 2–3 (1984), p. 114. The translation of this passage by J. D. Gauthier S. J. has been extensively modified [Trans.].

25. Ibid., p. 123. Translation slightly modified.

26. Jean Robelin's La Rationalité de la politique (Paris: Annales Littéraires de l'Université de Besançon/Les Belles Lettres, 1995) contains a remarkable formulation of the incompleteness of politics and the ensuing aporia in the idea of 'the transformation of social relations' as mastery of a totality.

27. Foucault, Dits et Écrits, IV, p. 587.

28. Le propre is, untranslatably, both that which is one's own and 'the clean', as perhaps produced by cleansing. [Trans.]

29. Fethi Benslama, 'La dépropriation', in Lignes, 24, February 1995, pp. 36, 39–40.

30. Gilles Deleuze and Félix Guattari, A Thousand Plateaus: Capitalism and Schizophrenia, trans. Brian Massumi (London: Athlone Press, 1988), pp. 291–2. [I have corrected one obvious misprint here, and put the term 'history' in the more usual lower case, since English does not have to mark the distinction between histoire (story) and Histoire (history) – Trans.].

31. Étienne Balibar, 'Violence: idéalité et cruauté', in La Crainte des Masses (Paris: Galilée, 1997); see also Chapter 7 below.

32. Bertrand Ogilvie, 'Violence et représentation. La production de l'homme jetable', in Lignes, 26, October 1995. [A more literal translation of 'poblacion chatarra' would be 'junk population' – Trans.].

33. Perhaps if Foucault could have seen the way African 'demography' is 'regulated' by the AIDS epidemic (and a number of other epidemics, all monitored by a 'World Health Organization'), he might have ventured to speak of 'negative bio-politics'.

34. This expression was coined by the psychoanalyst André Green. See La Folie privée. Psychanalyse des cas-limites (Paris: Gallimard, 1990), pp. 287ff.

35. These theses are, in part, condensed versions of analyses made in other

essays. See Étienne Balibar and Immanuel Wallerstein, *Race, Nation, Class: Ambiguous Identities* (London: Verso, 1991); 'Internationalisme ou barbarie', in *Lignes*, 16, 1992. See also, in this volume, Chapter 3, 'Ambiguous Identities'.

36. A word can be justified only by its usage, and this includes the contexts in which it is used. I choose the term civility for its dual relationship with citizenship (*civilitas* was the Latin translation of *politeia*; the French word '*civilité*' was first introduced by Nicolas Oresme in the sense of 'the institution or government of a community', and hence as synonymous with what we call 'politics' – as indeed was the English term 'civility') and with morals, public and private (the sense of the Hegelian term *Sittlichkeit*). I prefer the term *civilité* to possible French alternatives, such as '*gouvernement*', '*police*' and '*politesse*'. I also prefer it to the term 'civilization' (in spite of the active use made of this term by Norbert Elias – both in *The Civilizing Process* (original, 1936) and other works – which is incontestably related to our concerns here, even though Elias is more interested in socialization than politics, and leans towards an interpretation of civilization as a training in inner and outer discipline). It should also be said that the term 'civilization' is not easily dissociated from the idea that there are barbarians and savages who have to be 'civilized' (that is to say, in practice, subjected to the worst violence).

37. Kant, again following St Paul (and Luther), writes: 'if he lives among others of his own species, man is *an animal who needs a master*'. Kant, 'Idea for a Universal History, Sixth Proposition', in *Political Writings*, p. 46.

38. On this point, Pierre Bourdieu rightly cites some uncompromising pages by Thomas Bernhard in *Old Masters*. See Étienne Balibar, 'La violence des intellectuels', in *Lignes*, 25, May 1995.

39. See Ogilvie, 'Violence et représentation', for a somewhat different reading of these same Hegelian analyses.

40. In Section IV B of that document, Marx writes: 'Im preussisch-deutschen Reich nun gar . . . bedarf . . . der Staat einer sehr rauhen Erziehung durch das Volk.' Marx/Engels, *Ausgewählte Schriften*, II (Berlin: Dietz Verlag, 1971), p. 26/ 'in the Prusso-German Empire of all places . . . it is . . . the State that could do with a rude education by the people'. Marx, 'Critique of the Gotha Programme', *The First International and After* (Harmondsworth: Penguin Books in association with New Left Review, 1974), p. 357. [Trans.].

41. Deleuze and Guattari, *A Thousand Plateaus*, p. 215.

(*Translated by Chris Turner*)

2

Is There Such a Thing as European Racism?[1]

The ideas I offer for discussion here arise in a particular place (the great financial and intellectual metropolis of the German Federal Republic) and at a particular time: in the aftermath of the atrocious attacks on the community of Turkish immigrant workers, but also following the first great demonstrations of a rejection of fascist, xenophobic violence in German cities. While keeping these conditions in mind, I shall pitch my thoughts at a more general level: not only because I do not want to treat superficially a situation which other, better-informed speakers will have presented from the inside, but because I am convinced that the present German situation, despite its historical specificity, in reality represents one component element of the European conjuncture. It seems to me that it is at this level that it can be understood and, in the last instance, dealt with.

I shall argue as follows:

• first, that the racism we are seeing intensify and spread throughout the European continent – East as well as West – has deep roots in our history, even if we should never present that history in terms of a linear determinism. The connections being established between the popular forms of this neo-racism and the activities of organized ultra-nationalist minorities give us just concern to fear the emergence of neo-fascism in Europe. The virtual hegemony of these movements within a sector of youth desocialized by unemployment is particularly serious;

- second, the question arises whether this dynamic is an autonomous phenomenon or whether it represents a reaction to a
  situation of arrested social development and political impotence.
  This second hypothesis seems to me to be the right one: racism
  and fascism in Europe today are the conjunctural effects of the
  insoluble contradictions into which, despite their apparent triumph, the neoliberal economy and, in particular, the so-called
  representative political system (which in reality 'represents' fewer
  and fewer of the electors) have sunk. Admittedly, the more these
  contradictions intensify, the more a self-destructive spiral arises,
  with unpredictable effects;
- third, I do not believe that this development, albeit very far
  advanced, is beyond the control of democratic forces, provided
  that they face up fully to the initiatives which have urgently to be
  developed at local and transnational levels. It seems to me
  realistic to argue that internal obstacles, which are for the
  moment insurmountable, currently prevent the pure and simple
  reproduction across Europe of a process akin to that which led to
  the political triumph of fascism and Nazism in the early years of
  the twentieth century. There is a 'window' for collective action,
  and we can and should strive to take advantage of it.

Let us examine the first point. The circumstances in which we find
ourselves three years after what some have called the 'revolution of
1989'[2] call for an unvarnished political diagnosis. In this we must
be brutally honest both about the society in which we live and about
ourselves, as those who – or so we fondly believe at times – represent
our society's critical consciousness. I say a political diagnosis, but a
moral diagnosis is involved as well: not in the sense of passing moral
judgements on reality, but in the sense that we need also to assess
moral capacities, and that a moral crisis is part of the present
historical situation. At the centre of that crisis stand feelings of
complacency, but also of horror and impotence – if not, indeed,
fascination – in the face of European racism. Now, the more urgent
the circumstances become, the more it is necessary coolly to assess
their reality and conceptualize them.

It is important, in particular, to ask ourselves what exactly is new, and what in reality is the continuation or reproduction of a situation which goes back a very long way. What is indisputably new is the intensification of violent and *collective* manifestations of racism; the 'acting out' which is, collectively and publicly, transgressing the taboo on murder, and thereby affording itself, even in forms which seem vulgar and primitive to us, the terrible good conscience of a historical right. The crossing of that threshold – or rather, of a series of successive thresholds in that direction – has occurred in one European country after another, the target always being generically the populations of 'immigrant workers' and 'refugees', in particular those from southern Europe and Africa, but also – and I shall come back to this – a part of the foreign European population – if not, indeed, of the national population – which shares the same social characteristics (essentially the status of *displaced, de-territorialized* persons). Over the past ten years or so, it has seemed as though the baton has passed from one country to another in a sort of process of negative emulation. The result is that no European country can claim immunity from this process: from East to West, from Britain and France to Italy, Germany, Hungary and Poland (I hardly dare mention the Yugoslav 'case' here). And on each occasion this intensification has been accompanied, with more or less close and confirmed links, by an advance on the part of organized ultra-nationalist groups and a resurgence of anti-Semitism – an essentially symbolic anti-Semitism, as Dan Diner stressed yesterday.[3] This is not, however, to downplay the seriousness of that anti-Semitism, since this proves that it is indeed the model to which xenophobic thinking refers, haunted as it is by the dream of a 'final solution to the question of immigration'.[4] On each occasion, opinion polls have revealed, to all who harboured the contrary illusion, that the arguments legitimating racism as a kind of defensive reaction to 'threats' to national identity and the security of society are accepted by broad strata in all social classes, even if their extreme forms do not (not yet?) meet with general approval. Particularly strong is the idea that the presence of a large number of foreigners or immigrants threatens standards of living, employment or public order, and the idea that some cultural differences – often, in reality, very small ones – constitute insurmountable obstacles to living alongside each other, and might even be in danger of 'denaturing' our traditional identities.

It is this entire picture which gives cause for concern, even fear (above all, let us remember, the fear of those personally targeted) and prompts comparisons with the situation in which fascist movements emerged in Europe in the 1920s and 1930s. Here there is without doubt a challenge of comparable seriousness, but not necessarily the challenge of the same historical processes. In order to establish precisely what we are dealing with, we should in my view seek, not to relativize this picture, but to *qualify* it more precisely – and we should do this in two ways.

On the one hand, we should stress that racism, in so far as it *first and foremost* targets populations of workers from the 'underdeveloped' – generally ex-colonial or semi-colonial – world (even potential workers, the category to which refugees belong), is a phenomenon which goes back a very long way in Europe, and this includes its violent forms. Immigrants in Europe have long been the 'lowest of the low'.[5] The phenomenon has merely become more visible since it has emerged from the main arena to which it was previously confined – the workplace, that is to say, the site of exploitation – and its more or less ghettoized immediate environment. But we must say right away that the visibility or spread of the phenomenon is in itself an aggravating factor, in particular when it contributes to sustaining a sense of mass insecurity, and to making criminal acts seem banal and commonplace – something it does with at least the passive assistance of the major media.

Furthermore (the second qualification), we have to stress that this highly ideologized racism remains, for all that, historically complex, if not indeed contradictory. It is directed both against groups of 'external' origin (extra-European groups, groups from outside the European Community, some of which, however, have long belonged to the European social space, and in this sense are, *with* their cultural differences, completely 'integrated' into it) and against groups of 'internal' origin (sometimes groups within the nation, such as the *terroni* of the Italian South, who are victims of racism in the North), who are typically lumped in with the confused or wilfully confusing category of immigrants or migrants. And it

projects itself simultaneously into mutually incompatible mythical
narratives – including chiefly those of anti-Semitism (which might
better be described once again as anti-Jewishness) and anti-Islamism
or anti-Africanism, or anti-Third-Worldism. This shows that, though
European identity is undoubtedly one of the imaginary factors in this
mass intolerance, it is in no sense the major underlying premiss.
Clearly, within the ideological horizon of current 'European racism', there is as much *a rejection of Europe* in a whole series of its
historical components (it therefore represents a way for Europeans
to reject each other mutually) as *an appeal to, or defence of, 'European
identity'*. Or – to take this hypothesis to its logical conclusion – we
have here not just a 'rejection of the other', stigmatized racially and
culturally, but equally an exacerbation of the perception of intra-
European differences and, in a sense, a 'self-racization' of Europe
in a new sense – directed *against itself.*

This point seems important, particularly in so far as our analyses
have to steer a careful course between, on the one hand, the
rejection of certain massive Eurocentric legacies, certain persistent
traces of European domination, beginning with the trace of slavery,
conquest, colonization and imperialism; and, on the other, the
adoption of simplistic Third-Worldist schemas. The object (the
target) of current European racism is not by any means just the
black, the *Arab* or the *Muslim*, though they doubtless bear the main
brunt. This point is also important because it forces us once again
to go beyond abstract interpretations in terms of *conflicts of identity*,
or *rejection of the Other* and of 'otherness' as such – as though
otherness were something constituted *a priori*: explanations which,
in reality, merely reproduce part of the racist discourse itself.

Having outlined these qualifications or complexifications, however, we must return to the elements of the overall picture which
justify the fear of a development of neo-fascism, and lead us to
think that we are going to have to face up to a long-term crisis that
is as much moral as it is social. Without going at length here into
the structural elements which relate to the economy and state
intervention, and without denying the importance of what Uli
Bielefeld[6] termed in a recent article a 'popular extremism of the

centre', I should like to mention two such elements which call for detailed analysis. And they may perhaps be indirectly linked.

The first lies in the spread – which might be described as potentially hegemonic (in the sense that it is capable of giving rise to a *social movement*) – of the spectre of the collective attitudes and ideological formations grouped around the theme (and sometimes the slogan) of rejection of the foreigner. More deeply yet – and more precisely – what we have here are the themes of the rejection of *foreignness*, of the passionate, hysterical denial of its cultural and historical function (in the sense in this case both of *Bildung* and of *Zivilisation*). This expresses itself mainly, in both popular and in academic discourse, in the downright projective obsession with a tide of foreigners and foreignness that is supposed to be assailing 'us' in the name of 'multiculturalism' and 'interbreeding'. It would seem essential to understand concretely, from genuine field studies, how this pure phantasm can become a mass phenomenon, and provide a discourse – and hence a consciousness – for all manner of displaced social conflicts.

The other element I wish to refer to here concerns the growing involvement of youth in manifestations of racism (mainly of 'marginal' youth, but this is a mass marginality which is tending towards becoming constitutive of the 'condition of youth' for entire social groups). We are going to have to ask ourselves once again what youth is – we who are no longer young – and the first thing we have to do, no doubt, is confess that we have no idea, despite the countless batteries of statistics at our disposal.[7] It would be dangerous to believe that what we have here is merely an *isolated* group (once again, it would be to take at face value the sense of marginality and exclusion expressed in the youth movements, including in the crucial, but complex, phenomenon of local gangs, which are not all inspired by the apeing of Nazism, even though they all rummage through the lumber room of European history for symbols of social exclusion and infamy). But it would be equally dangerous to deny that, whether we like it or not, racist actions, or actions relating only indirectly to identity-claims, are perhaps the *only actions* today that bring about political 'gatherings' of youth *as such*. In Europe, there have never been organized liberal youth movements; there are no longer any communist or socialist or pacifist youth movements; apart from a few exceptional cases, there are very few ecological or Christian youth movements. On the other hand, there are virtually neo-fascist youth organizations, and this is very worrying politically. History is not made by middle-aged people.

This observation brings us to my second point, which I shall deal with at much less length: what are the historical trends indicated in these social phenomena, in which, of course, we fully include the ideological phenomena of collective contagion? In simple terms, since I have felt compelled to speak of potential hegemony: is this a movement or a convergence of movements with a 'grass roots' of its own, or is it 'merely' (though this does not necessarily make things any easier) a *reactive* movement, a riposte to certain apparently insoluble contradictions? As I have said, I opt for this latter hypothesis – or, rather, wish to submit it for discussion here. Not because I want at all costs to adhere to a classic Marxist schema, but for two precise reasons.

First, the phenomenon of *exclusion* (and the awareness of being 'excluded' or the fear of becoming so, or merely the refusal to live together with those who are excluded) clearly occupies a central place in the current racist syndrome. And whether we like it or not, this stands in a direct relation to a massive economic base (which includes the *state*, which consists not so much of lasting 'structures' as of a determinate economic policy). *Who* is excluded, and what are the 'excluded' excluded from? To answer these questions is both to unpack the concrete conditions for all the confusion and ambivalence we have identified in the targets of neo-racism (including the part that may be played by a process of self-racization) and to point, in the last analysis, to the principal contradiction in the current conjuncture, which I shall term *the regressive expansion of the market* in our society. Let us understand by this that the slogan and project of the universalization of market relations and of the corresponding social norms (in certain cases, we can go so far as to speak, paradoxically, of a *plan* systematically to eliminate all obstacles to the market) leads not to a real *growth* of the capitalist economy, but to *growing* deindustrialization and structural unemployment. This, we should note, is in no sense a phenomenon which solely characterizes the *Abwicklung* of the countries of the former Soviet Union.

Is the development of productivity really the essential cause of this, as we are so often told? Should we not, rather, seek its origins in the economic contradiction which consists in attempting to build a monetary and financial fortress in an isolated European space, the intention being to transform that space into a protected market and a reserve for highly remunerative capital (a kind of large-scale Switzerland)? And also – perhaps most importantly – in the fact that the expansion of capitalist production and commodity consumption cannot be achieved today by reaching back beyond the forms of social representation and collective participation which were won over a period of a century and more by the workers' movement? Growth (whatever its *qualitative* and qualitatively *new* modalities) could be said, rather, to require a *widening* of those forms of representation and participation, which in practice means a more balanced social compromise, an increase in the collective power and individual initiative of the workers in the broad sense of the term. But this is precisely what the current 'power elites' refuse even to contemplate – for reasons which are more *political* than technical. And it is what the old labour-movement organizations were incapable of conceiving, demanding, and organizing.[8] To put it plainly: exclusion has meaning only in relation to the arrested development and regression of the national-social state (I use this term as a realist equivalent of the mythical notion of the Welfare State).

But this brings me to a second reason which is, in reality, merely the corollary of the first. If the national-social state is torn between the world financial market and the regressive management of domestic social conflict, its own political crisis is developing in a relatively autonomous way. The paradox of this crisis is that it presents itself both as a crisis of existing states (crisis of effectiveness, crisis of legitimacy) and as a crisis of that *nonexistent* state which is the ideal end-goal of the construction of Europe.[9] It is towards that nonexistent state (or rather, towards the bureaucracy which stands in for it, a bureaucracy subject to the fluctuations of local political interests yet free from any real public control) that an increasing number of institutional and economic decisions have shifted. But that state, which is in reality a non-state, is clearly incapable of defining for itself (and, quite simply, of contemplating) a social base, founded upon a representation and a mediation of collective conflicts, comparable to the representation and mediation which had gradually come to bestow legitimacy upon democratic nation-states.

Failure to analyse this paradox, which generates the grotesque ongoing spectacle of an antisocial social state, of anti-national national states (in spite of periodic symbolic manifestations of sovereignty which, like French participation in the Gulf War, rebound on themselves) and, finally, the spectacle of a 'supra-national' state dead set against any form of popular or collective internationalism, would, as I see it, prevent us from understanding the way the themes of exclusion, corruption, and also political impotence combine today in the perception of the crisis of the state.

I have attempted elsewhere to point out the paradoxical psycho-logical effects of the phenomenon of the political and social impotence of a state which is proliferating administratively, and overequipped with security apparatuses which play a role at all levels in the way questions of collective insecurity, the integration of migrants or the reception of refugees fuel popular racism.[10] But I also stress this point to highlight the limits of the analogy with the rise of fascism. European fascism, particularly Nazism, arose in part as a reaction against *the collapse of the state* under the impact of defeat and civil war, not against a generalized sense of its impo-tence. On the contrary, it was, in its way, a component part of a phase of *apotheosis of the state*, to which all regimes and political ideologies contributed at the time, and to which it brutally sub-jected its own 'totalitarian mass movement'. The existing state may perhaps collapse in some parts of (Eastern) Europe, but what we see more generally is the manifestation of its impotence (first and foremost, the state's impotence to transform, reform and regenerate itself). The difference from historical fascism, even if there are fascist tendencies and movements today, is that no force can build up a political discourse of hegemonic pretensions around a programme of *strengthening the state*, or increased centralization of the state. Similarly, I think I am able to argue that no force can pull together identity-based demands in Europe around a *univocal* nationalism.

The fact remains that nationalism(s), racism(s) and fascism(s) represent a spectrum of ideological formations which, in a sense, presuppose each other. But this leads only to the phantom of an integral, integrative nationalism. Just as the social crisis is crystalliz-ing around a nonexistent state – I would suggest: around the absence of a state or of *the idea* of a state – so European racism is forming for itself multiple identity-based reactions which occupy the place of an *impossible nationalism* (and, as a consequence, obsessionally mimic its symbols at different levels).

I shall now close with an interpretative hypothesis and a proposal for intervention – not, of course, a programme, but a suggested approach. If I am at least partially right in the description I have presented so far, this means that the current European conjuncture, worrying as it is, is not an expression of an unambiguous trend or, even less, of a catastrophic determinism. It is simply the expression – though this in itself is a very serious matter – of the demand for a radical refoundation and a renewal of the – necessarily collective – democratic practices which are capable of breaking the vicious circle of European construction *from below*, and hence procuring for the political institution as such the possibility of a *new stage* – necessarily in the direction of its democratization or, to put it another way, in the direction of a limitation of the privileges and extension of the rights which constitute citizenship.

The European conjuncture will, for a certain time, remain in suspense, even if the situation is becoming increasingly tense. I am prompted to propose this – relatively optimistic, but *conditional* – hypothesis by the fact that it seems to me that one can identify a considerable gap between the exacerbation of the phenomena of exclusion and political demoralization which fuel the European expansion of racism, and the capacities of any political movement generally to group social and identity-based demands around the rejection of foreigners. Such a movement of rejection is, therefore, condemned to remain internally divided, and in this sense to neutralize itself, as it were, both within each country and at the European level, which is increasingly the horizon of our political practice. Unfortunately, this in no way diminishes its destructive capacities. And we know, or ought to know – unless we cover our eyes, we can *see* it at our gates – that 'barbarism' is always a possible alternative. But in this gap, this political 'window', the possibility for an intellectual and moral alternative based on anti-racism – that is to say, on *the rejection of the rejection of the other* – is undoubtedly still possible.

After the very interesting contributions we have heard, in spite of their divergences (or thanks to those very divergences), I should like to make the following point, and connect it to the themes of the multicultural society and citizenship.

I have said that what seemed most worrying to me in the present situation – as a *European* situation tending to spread to all countries (each country having reached this point by different routes) – was the potential hegemony of a neo-fascist ideology among young people who are objectively victims of exclusion, whether it be exclusion from work and consumption (pauperization), the exclusion from status and recognition which always goes with it, or, quite simply, exclusion from any future prospects. For young people in that position, 'citizenship' is an empty word and, as a consequence, 'democracy' is in danger of becoming so too, not to mention 'human rights'. Forgive me for employing rather old-fashioned language here, though I mean this in militant rather than military terms: I am convinced that this is the main terrain on which we must do battle. Young people with no prospects are, without any doubt, looking for solidarity, for community: they are, therefore, in search of an *identity* – or, rather, they are in search of ways and forms in which *to identify themselves*.

This means they are in no way seeking to preserve, reconstruct or recover a culture in the quasi-ethnographic sense of the term –

in the sense of a *way of life*, a set of rites and customs which make up a *Lebenswelt*. In actual fact, they hate their *Lebenswelt* and their culture in this sense. Or, alternatively, we should understand 'culture' [*Kultur*] in the sense in which Freud spoke of *Das Unbehagen in der Kultur*,[11] in the sense of civilization. The excluded youth of today, objects of potential manipulation by neo-fascism or, rather, potential objects of self-manipulation – including the exacerbated forms of English, Scottish, German (or, rather, 'West German' and 'East German'), northern Italian or southern Italian nationalism, and so on – are not, fundamentally, in search of cultures; they are looking for *ideals* – and they naturally seek these in symbols, which may at times take the form of fetish-objects. Old Marxist, old materialist that I am, I am convinced on this point: the main way of being a materialist, a realist, in politics today is to be 'idealistic' or, more precisely, to raise the question of ideals and the choices to be made between ideals. These ideals will necessarily be new expressions of very old ideas to which democracy appeals, but of which democracy, in its current manifestations, provides a very sad spectacle – ideas which are translatable both at the economic level and at that of symbolic recognition. I am thinking above all here, initially, of the idea of the *equality* of citizens; secondly, of the idea of the *truth* of political discourse; and, thirdly, of the idea of *security*, understood as the reduction of violence and the 'role of violence' in politics – by which I obviously do not mean repression or, in other words, counter-violence.[12] These are probably the three things most seriously lacking in our current constitutional states.

With this, however, we can attempt to shift the debate on multiculturalism a little. This seems to me currently to be locked into an absurd alternative. Let me say, more modestly, that I fear it may be locked into an absurd alternative. And this is so, once again, on account of the intrinsic ambivalence of the very idea of culture. I can well understand how useful it may be to speak of a multicultural or multiethnic society (as Daniel Cohn-Bendit and Claus Leggewie do[13]) in a country like Germany, where the idea of cultural homogeneity, of the *Kulturnation*, has official status, and is incorporated into the institutions and the law of the *Staatsnation* – for example into the conditions for naturalization [*Einbürgerung*].

Contrary to a legend deeply entrenched on both sides of the Rhine, it is not certain that France represents an absolutely opposite case. But, however that may be, this ought to lead us to deconstruct this notion, to demonstrate that there is in Europe *no* national culture which is 'homogeneous', particularly not so-called 'German culture'. The aim cannot be, then, to induce a particular 'national culture' more or less peacefully to regard itself, on its own, imaginarily closed-off territory, as *one culture among others* – or, in other words, to pass, as it were, from cultural monism to cultural pluralism.

Once again, what are in play here are not customs or traditions, but symbolic demarcation lines, and these demarcation lines are registered in institutions, in the architecture and practice of massive state apparatuses; while they are also overdetermined by rifts in social and economic conditions. The order of the day, then, in my view, is to *disrupt the dialogue* between 'civil society' and the 'state', which has for some time now – at least at the level of public consciousness and discourse – been a dialogue between *cultural communities* and the state in which politics disappears, and *to reintroduce a third term: the political movement* (I use this term advisedly, rather than party or organization).

We must aim for a recognition by institutions – by the state at its different levels – of *existing* 'cultural difference', both individual and communal (and the state runs from the level of a local authority, a housing authority or a school right up to supra-national administrative bodies). In France, for example, we must demand an end to discrimination against the Islamic religion in the name of official 'laicity' (which Edgar Morin has quite rightly dubbed 'Catholaicity'). But we must *at the same time* – and this, I believe, is the precondition for everything else – reconstitute a *demos* for democracy: *das Volk*, not '*ein Volk*', as the Leipzig demonstrators initially proclaimed five years ago. In simple terms, this means creating democratic, civic (but not state) movements, and in particular *transcultural* movements (and even transcultural cultural movements) – both movements which *cut across cultural borders* and movements which *reach beyond* the viewpoint of cultural identities, that is to say, which make possible, and embody, other forms of identification.

The question I pose, then, is whether this twofold objective – of enshrining a recognition of the 'right to difference' in state institutions, and of developing political and civic movements facing the state (which does not mean *against* it: *dem Staat gegenüber, nicht dem Staat entgegen*) – can be achieved today *within the national* (or purely national) *framework*. I do not have the time fully to justify my position here, but I think it is, in fact, impossible, and that the only level at which there is a chance (I do not say a certainty) of succeeding in this is the European level: the level of an open, transnational European citizenship, which is to be discussed and defined as it develops its social bases, its ideology. The question of a European culture does not even arise (except in the nostalgic dreams of Pope John Paul II), and the culture of a European nation or super-nation has no meaning; that includes culture on the American model – indeed, particularly, such a model. On the other hand, a task which does lie before us today is the construction of a European public space, a European *Öffentlichkeit*. And we are precisely deploying our intellectual resources here to develop such a thing.

This construction of a public space or a space of European citizenship is on the agenda because, *pace* Dahrendorf, *there was no revolution in Europe in 1989*; because the European project of central banks and bureaucracies is politically dead; but also because it is impossible and unbearable to allow ourselves to be locked into a choice between this corpse or a return to nineteenth-century nationalisms – indeed, medieval nationalisms, if it is true that in a few years there may no longer be a British or an Italian nation-state.

In this long march towards the European public space – a march which is also a race – we can clearly see that the intervention of the members of the Turkish communities or pseudo-communities in Germany, of Indians and Pakistanis in Britain, of Arabs or Africans in France, and so forth, is an essential moment. These groups, which are today objects of demagoguery and obsessional fixation, will tomorrow be fully fledged political actors. But this will be so only if they do not remain 'among their own kind', and we do not remain 'among our own kind'. When something like a march, a congress, a demonstration or a network of European youth for democratic rights and equality emerges, then at that point we shall be able to say that a door has opened.

Notes

1. Paper delivered at the Congress 'Fremd ist Fremde nur in der Fremde', Frankfurt am Main, 11–13 December 1992, organized by Friedrich Balke, Rebekka Habermas, Patrizia Nanz, Peter Sillem and Fischer Verlag (published in German as *Schwierige Fremdheit. Uber Integration und Ausgrenzung in Einwanderungsländern*, Fischer Taschenbuch Verlag, 1993), and in Étienne Balibar, *La Crainte des masses. Politique et philosophie avant et après Marx*, (Paris: Galilée, 1997).

2. Ralf Dahrendorf, *Reflections on the Revolution in Europe* (London: Chatto & Windus, 1990).

3. Dan Diner, 'Nationalstaat und Migration. Zu Begriff und Geschichte', in *Schwierige Fremdheit*, pp. 21 ff.

4. In the recent attitudes of certain groups which have carried out pogroms, this regression becomes explicit, but it is also explicit in the German government's attitude towards gypsies.

5. *Lowest of the Low* is the title of the English translation by Martin Chalmers (London: Methuen, 1988) of Günther Wallraff's *Ganz Unten*.

6. Uli Bielefeld, 'Populärer Extremismus der Mitte. Die neuen Legitimations probleme in Deutschland', *Frankfurter Rundschau*, 5 December 1992.

7. The presence of François Dubet here is – for me, at least – a guarantee that some people are asking the question: see F. Dubet, *La Galère, jeunes en survie* (Paris: Fayard, 1987; reprinted Paris: Seuil, 1995).

8. See Jean-Louis Moynot, *Au milieu du gué. CGT, syndicalisme et démocratie de masse* (Paris: PUF, 1982). At the time Moynot was secretary general of the French CGT union.

9. Étienne Balibar, '*Es gibt keinen Staat in Europa*: racisme et politique dans l'Europe d'aujourd'hui', in *Les frontières de la démocratie* (Paris: La Découverte, 1992), pp. 169–90/'*Es gibt keinen Staat in Europa*: Racism and Politics in Europe Today', *New Left Review*, 186, March/April 1991, pp. 5–19.

10. Balibar, 'Racisme, nationalisme, État', in *Les frontières de la démocratie*, pp. 79–95.

11. Freud's work of this title was, of course, translated into English as *Civilization and its Discontents* [Trans.].

12. See Étienne Balibar, '. . . "la sûreté et la résistance à l'oppression". Sûreté, sécurité, securitaire', in *Cahiers Marxistes* (Brussels), 200, November–December

1995. Reprinted in Balibar, *Droit de cité: culture et politique en démocrati,* (Paris: Éditions de l'aube, 1998), ch. 3, pp. 27–42.

13. Claus Leggewie, *Multi Kulti. Spielregeln für die Vielvölkerrepublik* (Berlin: Rotbuch Verlag, 1993). See also his paper to the Frankfurt congress, 'Vom Deutschen Reich zur Bundesrepublik – und nicht zurück. Zur politischen Gestalt einer multikulturellen Gesellschaft', in *Schwierige Freiheit.*

(Translated by Chris Turner)

3

Ambiguous Identities[1]

In the space of a few years or months, the question of nationalism, which seemed merely a matter of historical interest, or appeared to survive in most regions of the world only as a remnant of a previous age (which amounts to much the same thing), has become the central question of politics and the social sciences. Around that question we have seen a proliferation of debates, diagnoses, publications and genealogies. While the ending of the great confrontation between East and West, which ranged virtually transnational world systems against each other, seemed necessarily to mark the 'end of ideologies', we are seemingly now approaching a point where, in every country, the crucial question will be whether one is for or against nationalism or, more exactly, for or against a particular form of nationalism or critique of nationalism. Where, not so long ago, the works of Marx, Keynes and Hayek were being pored over, it is now the theorists of cultural and political nationalism – Herder, Fichte, Mazzini, Renan – who are studied in the search for keys to historical interpretation.

At the same time, though it is not easy to say which is cause and which effect, economic and social forms of explanation (including the Marxian theory of classes and class struggle) and the politico-juridical theories of democracy and the *Rechtsstaat*, and so on, are either pushed into the background or called upon to account for the national and nationalist 'phenomenon'.

With this displacement of the ideological scene, there is one
word we now encounter everywhere. That word is *identity*. The
prototype of identity is, it seems, national – if not, indeed, 'ethnic'
– identity. All sociology is becoming, or reverting back to, the
sociology of identities (in other words, it is becoming, or reverting
back to, psychosociology): linguistic identities, religious identities,
class identities. And the great question of the moment is how these
various identities present obstacles – or add dimensions – to
national identity.

I myself am, therefore, also going to attempt to propose the
outlines of an analysis of identities – or rather, of the very concept
of collective identity. In so doing, my central argument will be,
paradoxically, that *there is no* identity which is 'self-identical'; that *all
identity is fundamentally ambiguous*. If these outlines are to be properly understood, however, some preliminary (if not, indeed, precau-
tionary) remarks are required on the very possibility of talking
somewhere in the world, in such a way that one will be listened to,
about nationalism. Furthermore, the search for a logic of the
ambiguities of identity will lead me to formulate some theoretical
propositions on the nation-form itself, and on current variations of
racism. In conclusion, I shall attempt to give my opinion on the
question which, implicitly, underlies many current debates: has the
nation/class alternative, the choice between nationalism and class
ideology (one of the main forms of which is socialism), entirely lost
its explanatory function and its historically discriminating value
today?

I

Let us begin by restating an obvious point, though one that is sadly
often forgotten: wherever one talks about nationalism, and however
one talks about it, one is necessarily in an awkward position, since
one is necessarily the bearer of a particular nationalism, and
potentially opposed to another. More than in other fields of ideology, there is no neutral position or discourse here, no way of being
'above the fray'. Every position is partial in both senses. It is partial

not merely as a stand *for or against* a particular nationalism, the nationalism of a particular nation, and hence, ultimately, for or against a particular nation itself (since, as we shall see, each nation is one with its own nationalism), but partial also as an attempt to *define* nationalism. We are already deep into ambiguity here since, on the one hand, there is an absolute formal similarity among all nationalisms, a uniformizing, competitive mimicry; and, on the other, every nation – or in other words, every nationalism – has an absolutely singular way of defining nationalism and, in particular, of projecting it on to others (nationalism is an essentially *projective* ideology). In these conditions, it is highly likely that any definition of nationalism will be unacceptable to its addressees, since it confronts them with their own misrecognition of themselves.

Does this mean that nationalism cannot be analysed *objectively*? No, undoubtedly it does not, any more than this would apply to any social phenomenon, since objectivity in this case does not mean the *a priori reduction* of nationalism to some 'material base' or 'psychological mechanism', but the historical study of its constitution, its particular forms and its interaction with other social phenomena. However, objectivity cannot be equated here with the mere presupposition of a universalistic standpoint. The *particularism* (or exceptionalism) displayed by each nationalism leads easily to the idea that the 'standpoint' required to analyse it must be a universalistic one; but it is immediately apparent that every nationalism has within it an element of universalism, a more or less messianic claim to universality, whereas every theoretical universalism (religious, scientific or social) always contains a hidden particularism.

The situation of Marxism is particularly interesting in this connection for the acuteness of the contradiction which shows up within it. In basing itself on a historical perspective – more particularly, the perspective of the class struggle – it might seem that Marxism could find the 'Archimedean point': the if not supranational, then at least extra-national, standpoint (a point of view simultaneously distant and yet internal to the movement of history) from which to get beyond mere mirror-play with nationalism. To do so is, in fact, a key issue for it, yet we know that the analysis and consideration of nationalism have been the real blind spot of historical, theoretical and practical Marxism. There are two reasons for this which are diametrically opposed: on the one hand, economism, which Marxism shares with its *frère ennemi* liberalism, and which causes it to regard any ideology, any subjective construction other than its own 'class consciousness', as a 'superstructure' (in a sense, the blindness of Marxism on the origins and development of nationalism is strictly correlative with its blindness regarding the mechanisms of class consciousness – which points to the need to study the two things together); on the other hand, there is the fact that all historical Marxisms, whether embodied in a party or a state, have, in the very forms of their internationalism, been steeped in nationalism in the broad sense (including the extended nationalism that is Western ethnocentrism or its antithesis, Third-Worldism).

I shall make a brief topical observation here, as we are currently, with the 'end of the Cold War', coming out of a period of confrontation between the two great rival blocs and ideological systems (the two 'world-views') which have dominated political analysis for two or even three generations. Each of these presented itself as supra-national, as an internationalism, for there was a liberal internationalism just as there was a socialist internationalism. It is, however, doubtful whether the 'blocs', inasmuch as they were mutually exclusive and organized around state constructions, found any other cement for their internationalism than an expanded, loosened-up form of nationalism. Liberal internationalism was in many respects a Western nationalism, just as socialist internationalism was a Soviet nationalism, each with its dissident movements.

This tells us something very important. Although nationalism was historically, institutionally and even 'organically' linked to a certain type of social and historical formation which we may call the nation-state (either as the reflection of its existence or as the precondition of its constitution), it can also operate on other scales: not just smaller, 'local' scales, whether at the level of administrative or cultural entities, but larger, 'global' scales, determined at once by tradition and the particular conjuncture. There are, at least in the contemporary world, both infra-national nationalisms and supra-national nationalisms, so to speak. This suggests that nationalism is both the expression of certain social structures *and*, in a relatively autonomous way, a specific *schema* of ideological constitution, of communal construction, of conflictual production and recognition of collective identities. However, the same example, forced upon us by current events (and we would make the same observations with regard to more specific nationalisms), shows that there is very seldom – perhaps never – a 'pure' nationalism, a functioning of the ideological schema of 'assembling [*rassemblement*]'[2] in a purely national – that is to say, a purely political – way.

Each of the two great supra-nationalisms was imbued, in its way, with religious messianism *and* class ideology or 'class consciousness', though not necessarily along the lines most usually recognized. For example, one of the difficulties which most often stands in the way of recognition of (North) American nationalism, both from the inside and from the outside, is the fact that it is a very powerful bourgeois class nationalism (the 'American Way of Life' or, in other words, the absolute primacy of competitive individualism and the dogma of its human superiority), at the same time as it constitutes a prime instance of the idea of the 'chosen people' (chosen to save the world and fight 'Evil'). We can see here that the *universalistic* components of nationalism are probably indissociable from relations which nationalism, as an ideological schema, maintains historically with other such schemas that seem opposed to it, such as religious, social or class universalism. And, to conclude this point, we might suggest that, paradoxically, the most purely 'national' internationalism, but also the least effective during the same period, has been that of the *third* potential supra-national entity, which has attempted to carve out a place for itself alongside the two we have already mentioned: the Third-Worldism of Nehru, Tito, Nasser and Nkrumah, as an alliance between all the political, economic and cultural 'national liberation' movements.

I have rehearsed these arguments at length as a way of hinting at another proposition. One of the great difficulties with which any analysis of nationalism is faced is what I shall call the interplay between invisible and (over-)visible nationalisms, which is inextricably entangled with the division between dominant and dominated nationalisms or, more precisely, between nationalisms which express and consolidate domination and those which express and consolidate resistance. Between these there is clearly – from the political and ethical viewpoint, and also from the standpoint of their historical role – a fundamental asymmetry. There is also necessarily some degree of imitation. It cannot be merely accidental, for example, that Black Americans' greatest effort to conceive of themselves as a 'national' movement like other liberation movements coincided with the Vietnam War and, generally, with the high-water mark of the imperial assertion of 'white' American nationalism.

Except where they come into conflict with each other, dominant or oppressive nationalisms are generally 'invisible' as nationalisms, at least to themselves; they present themselves, rather, as political and cultural universalisms in which religious and economic components may coexist. Conversely, one is tempted to say that, at least in a certain period, nationalisms of political and cultural resistance to imperial, colonial or foreign central domination are generally 'over-visible' in that, on the one hand, they are generally blind to those causes and determinations that do not stem from the problem of the nation, and, on the other, they tend to subsume within themselves, particularly by way of the category of culture or 'cultural identity' – as a metaphor for national identity – all the other ideological schemas, both social and religious. It is true that this can change. The fact that, in the present conjuncture, many of the world's national movements are moving from a secular to a religious register is undoubtedly both the symptom of a great shift in the present conjuncture, a crisis of the dominant representations of politics (in which *all* identity-based movements, including the longest-standing, will have to redefine themselves), and proof that the *relationship* between the social and communal components, and between the different communal schemas, is never established once and for all, despite what might have been thought in the name of a certain ideology of 'modernity', itself closely linked to the dominant nationalisms.

II

What these considerations show is that the first task facing us is not to judge nationalisms and nationalism in general, but to understand it or, in other words, rationally to analyse its specificity. And, though it cannot be dissociated from researching into the causes of nationalism in the course of history and in a particular conjuncture, this task cannot simply be reduced to such research. It has a philosophical or anthropological dimension to it, which concerns, above all, the specifically national pattern of community or the mode of subjective identification which links the constitution of the individual personality to the nation, to national institutions or to the idea of nation.

The question of the *judgement* to be passed on nationalism in a particular conjuncture is clearly unavoidable in practice. This much I conceded above when I referred to the difference between dominant and dominated nationalisms. One might further illustrate it by reference to the current constitution of a 'European' nationalism. Nationalism in general, nationalism as such, is neither good nor bad; it is a historical form for interests and struggles which are *opposite in character*. But the conjuncture requires that we make choices. And these choices are often difficult, because the dominant, 'hegemonic' nationalisms may include a non-negligible gain in terms of universalism (what they themselves term 'civilization'), while the dominated nationalisms, whether ethnic or religious in tone, inevitably include a tendency towards exclusivism, if not indeed to actual exclusion, all the greater for the fact that they are fighting against uniformity. This is why it is important to have at our disposal instruments of analysis which are not neutral, but comparative.

As for the question of causes – of why, in a particular conjuncture (for example, in Europe today, from West to East) national movements are multiplying at all levels – this brings us back, in the last analysis, to the question of the *historicity of the nation-state* and the nation-form itself. It is impossible to expound the argument fully here (I have attempted to do so elsewhere[3]), but it is necessary to take a stand on a number of major issues. After the great debates of the nineteenth century, the question of what relationship pertains between *state* and *nation* is currently receiving renewed attention in an entirely new context characterized by an internationalization or 'globalization' which initially affects economic life and communication systems, the circulation of goods, people and information, but is also extending inevitably to military apparatuses, legal systems, and so on.

What do we see? A renewed tendency to regard nation-building as (or as potentially) relatively independent of the construction of the state, but this tendency takes two opposing forms. On the one hand, we have a proposal to dissociate 'citizenship' more or less completely from 'nationality' (in other words, to separate the right to politics [*droit à la politique*] from exclusive membership of a nation-state). On the other, the contention is that 'the nation should be separated from the state' in a manner comparable, *mutatis mutandis*, to the 'separation of Church and State'. We can see, here, that these are, in the end, opposing perspectives, the latter being formally conservative (globalization at last makes it possible for nations to acquire their autonomy, as cultural entities, from states), the former formally progressive (globalization will once and for all reduce the importance of the exclusive criterion of nationality, not just in the economic and cultural spheres, but also in politics).

In reality, it is not certain that the notion of nation-building is understood in an unambiguous sense here. This is what makes it all the more necessary, in my view, to reaffirm the historical connection between the form of the nation (and hence of the national 'community' and ideology, or nationalism) and a certain form of state (which we may term *bourgeois*, provided that we do not take this notion to be identical to that of a pure *capitalist* state. I shall come back to this point). The transformation of the nation-form and the relativization of the nation-state cannot, then, consist of a mere separation: they necessarily entail a redefinition, a recomposition – both of the state itself (the history of the state is not at an end, contrary to the beliefs of such very great minds as Hegel and Marx and such very limited ones as Fukuyama) and of society (or, if the reader prefers, of the community and the collectivity as forms and sites of 'the political').

To say that nationalism is, generically, the organic ideology of the nation-state or, more precisely, of the *age* of the nation-state as dominant form, is not to say that all nationalisms are statist, any more than all ideologies and religious movements were so in an earlier age. Nor is it to say that the bourgeois state operates only on the basis of nationalism. It is, however, to say that all nationalisms stand *in a relation to* the nation-state. That is to say, they serve it, contest it or reproduce it. And this makes nationalism the fundamental agent of the spread of this form, which, as we know, is in no way imposed everywhere at the same time, or in the same way, by the capitalist *economy*. It is also what enables us to understand why nationalism changes scale – why 'infra-nationalisms' and 'supra-nationalisms', viable or otherwise, are still nationalisms.

What do we mean when we talk about the *historicity of the nation-form*, or of the form of the nation-state? Essentially, we are talking about two things which go hand in hand.

First, there have in history been *other* state *forms* and even, potentially, other 'bourgeois' state forms (such as the city-state or the empire). And the problem of such alternatives in no sense belongs to the past: the same forms, transformed to a greater or lesser extent, are reappearing today as 'meta-national' forms. Moreover, there has in history been *more than one* route to the building of nations – routes leading to the 'nationalization' of society by the state. And there is still a great divide between the 'nations' of the centre and the 'nations' of the global periphery. But this divide (which renders problematic the unambiguous use of the term 'nation' as the name for a social formation) merely serves to highlight even more the hegemony of the 'central' form.[4] It is, precisely, the paradox of historical 'liberation' and 'development' movements that they have sought to abolish this division by making the periphery (or, to use Wallerstein's terminology, the 'semi-periphery') the new field for the expansion and regeneration of the central form itself.

Second, this form is neither something natural, nor something stable (not to say fixed). It is a process of reproduction, of permanent *re-establishment* of the nation. The nationalization of society to which we have referred – the administrative (decentralization/ centralization), economic and cultural (mainly schooling-related) aspects of which we could describe – presents itself historically as a task that can never be completed. The nation is, ultimately, an *impossible* entity, which can never entirely achieve its ideal, and it is as such – that is to say, as a problem – that it is *real*. An impossible task culturally, for 'multi-ethnicism' and 'multiculturalism' are present from the outset and are constantly re-forming themselves.[5] An impossible task economically, since the 'integral distribution' of human beings and resources between national units is in no sense a tendency of capitalism: at most, it is a means of its political 'reproduction' or its 'hegemony' (which once again underlines the distinction between the theoretical notions of *capitalism* and *bourgeois* society or domination).

In these conditions, the nationalization of society is a process of specific statization. But it is also a *compromise* – not just a more or less stable compromise between classes, but a compromise between the two 'principles' themselves: between the principle of nationality and that of class struggle. This is the first great factor of ambiguity in national identities and class identities, and a corollary of their reciprocal determination.

Nowhere is this ambiguity more apparent than in the joint crisis of these identities we are seeing today. Let us remain, for the moment, at the centre of the system: the effects of globalization can be felt everywhere, but it is at the centre (where the effects of social polarization and pauperization are to some degree suspended, where 'man does not live by bread alone' – or by oil) that the ideological dimension shows itself most prominently. The political crisis (which the end of the East–West confrontation is going to open up, and which is going to arise in 'the construction of Europe' around the crucial question: *what is the people? – Is there a European people*, and not just a European bank or European borders?) is not merely a crisis of the state in general, nor even of the 'bourgeois state' we have just referred to. It is a crisis of the ultimate form assumed by that 'bourgeois state' which has been referred to as the '*Welfare State*' or, in French, '*l'État-Providence*' (religion and economy once again), and which ought more rigorously to be described as the *national-social state*. In other words, it is a crisis of the relative integration of the class struggle, and classes themselves, into – and by – the nation-form. This is why it is properly a crisis of *hegemony* in Gramsci's sense, in which phenomena of class decomposition (both from above and from below) *and* phenomena of vacillating national identity occur, leading to some potent nationalist reactions (I would prefer to say: potent reactions on the part of nationalism, character-ized by the fact that the 'dominant' nationalisms themselves become defensive in this process and, thus, internally aggressive).

III

We may now return to the problem of identity and its national pattern. Is there, properly speaking, a mode of constitution of individual and collective identity that is specifically national?

We must, I think, study this question at the deepest level: not at the level of the mere discourses of the community (mythical, historical or literary grand narratives), nor even the level of collec-tive symbols or representations,[6] but the level of the *production of individuality* itself. In what way is the national-form linked to the production of a certain type of 'human being' (and of being a human being in the world), which we might term *Homo nationalis* (alongside *Homo religiosus, Homo oeconomicus*, etc.)? Or, in more philosophical language, what is the relationship of self to self, conscious and unconscious, involving both the individual person-ality and the community, which here produces the sense of *belonging* in the three senses of the term (the individual's belonging to the community, but also – and this is no less essential, as the theme of 'national preference' shows – the community's belonging to individ-uals and to 'national' groups, and hence the mutual sense of belonging between individuals)?

We must stress once again, against 'holistic' or 'organicist' myths, that every identity is *individual*. But every individuality is more than individual, and other than individual. It is immediately *transindividual*, made up of representations of 'us', or of the relation between self and other, which are formed in social relations, in daily – public and private – activities. To see this, one need only look back to Althusser's description of the family or of schooling (the great 'ideological state apparatuses').

In this connection, I shall put forward three fundamental ideas:

1. There is no *given* identity; there is only *identification.* That is to say, there is only ever an uneven process and precarious constructions, requiring symbolic guarantees of varying degrees of intensity.

Identification comes from others, and continues always to depend on others. Who are these others? How do they 'respond'? And are they even in a position to respond? (Here, material conditions – for example, conditions of social inequality and exclusion – have their full impact.) But this loop of identity has as a precondition – and operates within – historical *institutions* (not just official, dominant institutions, but also revolutionary institutions: this is why 'anti-systemic movements' equip themselves with anti-institutions to constitute their 'identity', anti-institutions on which their sustainability and relative autonomy depend).[7]

Institutions *reduce* the multiplicity or complexity of identifications. But do they suppress that multiplicity in such a way as to constitute one single identity? It seems to me that one can assert that this is 'normally' *impossible,* even though it is, just as 'normally', *required.* There is a *double-bind* here. This is where the basis of the problem of 'multicultural' (multinational, multireligious, etc.) society lies: not simply in the pluralism of the state, but in the oscillation for each individual between the two equally impossible extremes of absolutely simple identity and the infinite dispersal of identities across multiple social relationships; it lies in the difficulty of treating oneself as different from oneself, in a potential relation to several forms of 'us'. Given this situation, a part, at least, of each person's identity seems *given.*

2. Identification, constrained in this way, itself oscillates constantly between two great modalities of behaviour, between two poles which are inseparable, but in a state of unstable equilibrium. We find the two combined in what the philosophy of history and the social sciences of the bourgeois epoch (that is to say, the

national epoch) have termed *culture*.[8] Now, any definition of culture always ultimately combines the same two categories of distinctive characteristics:

- customary or *ritual* characteristics: this is the element of imaginary 'similarity', exhibiting the individual's belonging to the community as a common, physical or spiritual, 'nature' or 'substance', allegedly manifested in the resemblance of outward appearance, behaviour and gesture;

- characteristics of belief or *faith*: this is the element of symbolic 'fraternity' which shows itself above all in the common response (which is not only the same for all, but is symbolically proffered in common) to a transcendent appeal: the call of God, the Fatherland, the Revolution and so on. This is generally mediated (transmitted, repeated and interpreted) by inspired, authorized voices which lay down where duty lies (which ultimately takes the form, for each individual, of his or her own voice, in the sense of an inner voice of 'conscience').

Now, in the case of national identity (or of nationalism in the generic sense), there are two basic ideological themes (giving rise to a constant elaboration of discourses and narratives specific to each 'people' or 'nation') corresponding to each of these poles:

- on the one hand (that of the imaginary or ritual), what I have termed *fictive ethnicity*: no nation rests historically on a 'pure' ethnic base, but every nation, through its institutions, constructs a fictive ethnicity which distinguishes it from others by perceptible (visible, audible, etc.) marks, by 'typical' or 'emblematic' behavioural traits, which may possibly be worked up into the aggravated form of criteria for exclusion;

- on the other, *patriotism* – that is to say, the nation as transcendent community, implying a common 'destiny', and at least implicitly linked to the idea of a transhistorical mission – the salvation of its members (which may be sublimated into a mission to save the whole of humanity, if need be 'from itself'), having as its corollary the duty of each individual to 'hand on' from generation to generation a symbol which is the country's 'own' (pre-eminently the symbol of the language, but also that of the national 'dream', etc.).[9]

These two poles, though quite different in nature, cannot really be separated, since each, in practice, 'guarantees' the other. But they can be unilaterally accentuated and exacerbated. In the one case we come, then, to that supplement of nationalism that is racism (be it pseudo-biological or cultural, 'differentialist' racism); in the other we come to religious or quasi-religious nationalism:[10] either the alliance of nationalism with a religion which is in effect a 'state religion', or the production of an imitation religion (in many respects, French 'secularism' is such a form). It is quite clear that these two 'excesses' may be equally dangerous in different situations (not to speak of their combination which, paradoxically, characterized Nazism).

3. But – and this is our third idea – given the constantly reactivated plurality of identification processes, there is in the last analysis no identity (particularly not as individual identity) without the establishment of a *hierarchy* of communal references (and, through this, of 'belonging': the servant cannot have two equal masters; he can only attempt to play on the two registers).

Establishing a hierarchy of communal references does not mean absorbing their diversity into the uniform structure of a single 'totalitarian' belonging. It means, rather, constituting what we may call – borrowing once again from Gramsci's vocabulary – a *hegemony* within ideology itself. Historically, in the modern era (which has its roots deep in the 'Middle Ages'), it seems that two ideological schemas (two patterns of 'total community' or, as Ernest Gellner puts it, of Terminal Court of Appeal[11]) and two alone could, in competitive and alternating fashion, become hegemonic in this way: the schema of religion (I am thinking here particularly of the great universal Western religions: Christianity and Islam) and that of nationalism.

Each of these allows for the construction of both a spiritual and a temporal edifice (in particular, the enshrining of 'rules' in a legal system), capable of incorporating rites and beliefs, and hence of creating a 'culture'. Each, in its own way, reconciles particularism with universalism, and produces a hierarchy of 'belongings' (and thus of communal identities) by forcing them – violently if need be

– to be transformed, *without being destroyed* (in precisely this respect they differ from totalitarian domination – if such a thing has ever completely existed: precisely because all lasting domination of distinct, and *a fortiori* antagonistic, social groups by an ideology requires *mediations*). Each of these schemas, competing historically with the other, prides itself on a particular political achievement: religion on pacifying the nations and the relations between them; nationalism on forcing religions to show tolerance.

If this presentation is correct, we would have, then, to rectify the error (suggested by a philosophy of history which is itself very closely linked to modern nationalism) which sees the destiny of ideologies as following a *linear* course. In the event, this takes the form of a process of gradual 'secularization' or 'disenchantment' of societies and politics, which in practice means the decline of religion to the advantage of nationalism. History is certainly irreversible, but it is not linear: the proof is that, before our very eyes, the crisis of hegemony of nationalism has just begun, whereas that of religion (or of the universalism of a religious type) is still ongoing – and will probably continue to be so.

IV

Let us sum up the argument so far, and draw some conclusions.

It is difficult to find an external standpoint from which to define nationalism, to analyse the transformation of its functions and its place in the world: hence the need to confront it from within, and produce an immanent critique. This was our first point.

The nation-form is historical through and through: this was our second point. But *that historicity itself has a history*: a history which takes us today from a classical configuration – characterized by the opposition between 'dominant' and 'dominated' nationalisms, and hence also by political struggles for and against the nationalization of society (taking the form of class resistance or resistance which is itself national, and seldom totally independent) – to a new configuration characterized by the crisis of the national-social state, where it exists, and – where it has never really existed (that is to say, in the periphery) – by the no doubt even more serious crisis surrounding the very *prospect* of its construction.[12]

My third and last point was the intrinsic ambiguity and ambivalence of identities. There is nothing natural in the area of identity: there is a process of identification or production of forms of human individuality in history – a process related to the always-already given transindividual 'community' – by way of the complementary paths of resemblance and symbolic vocation. And this leads us to note the irreducible plurality of the great ideological schemas of construction of communal identity (or 'total' ideologies).

On this basis, we might attempt to situate historically a phenomenon such as current racism or neo-racism, particularly in the West and specifically in Europe. Even if, unarguably, nationalism is not identical to racism, racism and neo-racism are phenomena *internal* to the current history of nationalisms, as colonial racism and anti-Semitism were in the past (and we still see active *traces* of these today in what is termed neo-racism). Unarguably, too, racism is one of the effects, and the most worrying symptom, of the crisis of the national-social state: it is linked to the exclusion of the 'new poor', lumped together with those among them who bear the stigmata of national or cultural exteriority (and also, secondarily, to resentment of those 'foreigners' who, despite institutionalized 'national preference', are integrating into bourgeois society). Lastly, it is a means, both real and phantasmatic, of their *preventive exclusion*.

In conclusion, racism clearly corresponds to a displacement of the identity system of nationalism (of the representations and discourses which enable it to produce identities and order them hierarchically) towards the pole of (fictive) ethnicity. But it also corresponds to a transnationalization of nationalism itself. Hence the exacerbation of claims of 'ethnic' difference both at the top and bottom of society: in France, anti-Americanism is combining with anti-Arab sentiment.[13] But this is occurring as part of a strange combination of particularism (the 'we' has to be purified) and nostalgic universalism (evoking the lost paradise of the West, of 'European civilization').

It is at this point that the question of the ambiguous relationship between national and class identities would seem to arise once again. I said they were disrupted, if not indeed destroyed, *together* by globalization. It is from within this context that we should view this question. The crisis of the nation-state, and exclusion-related phenomena, are occurring as aspects of an extraordinarily contradictory change in world history: for the first time a humanity effectively unified (economically and technologically), *in immediate communication* from one end of the planet to the other (including militarily), has begun to exist. But for the first time, also, social polarization is assuming the form of a worldwide division between rich and poor, a disparity in wealth within a single social formation. There are no longer any *external* exclusions; the trend is solely towards *internal* exclusions. But they are dramatic exclusions, so violent that they revive and widely disseminate naturalistic representations of the superman and the subhuman. And we have not even mentioned all those who are *unsure of their place* (now and, crucially, in the future): the foot soldiers of every 'populism'.

Class consciousness has never been wholly separate from nationalism. Although it was intended to be an alternative, it has in fact been imbued with it (the history of the USSR and of 'real socialism' in general provides a dramatic illustration of this). Class consciousness maintains an ambivalent relationship even with racism. On the one hand (a historical aspect which is too often underestimated), 'proletarian' class consciousness was a militant reaction to the positive class racism directed at European workers in the nineteenth century (which is still with us today). *Internationalism* took some of its foundations (and the sources of its practical humanism) from the struggle against the excessive (i.e. racist) forms of nationalism itself. On the other hand, class consciousness is itself imbued with a sense of identity which is formally akin to racism: the fetishism and rites of *class origin*. Hence its vulnerability to xenophobia and the theme of the foreign threat (exploited by the ruling classes).

The days of *working-class* internationalism are doubtless now past, whether by that we mean state internationalism or, even, that of political parties (even if important corporatist aspects still exist, or may possibly re-form as part of the international convergence of trade-union interests). However, the need for an internationalist reaction to the explosion of – defensive/aggressive – 'crisis nationalisms' is clear. And in very large measure, the crisis of the national-social state derives from the total misadaptation of that historical structure when it comes to 'regulating' a social antagonism on a world scale, or constructing political mediations within the field of a global proletarianization contemporaneous with the effective globalization of capitalism. For some years now, scattered efforts to construct a *post-national* political internationalism or universalism seem to have been made within and among peace movements, anti-racist groups and even ecological movements (in the sense of an ecologism concerned not just with nature, but with the economy and power relations). Such an internationalism, however, would not be founded directly on a 'class base', seeking mythically and messianically to express a class identity. Even if it retained a class content and a sense of class struggle, its form would necessarily be independent of class, and would thus have to find a political identity for which there is as yet no name.

Notes

1. Contribution to the ninth *Semana Galega de Filosofia*, Pontevedra (Galicia), 20–24 April 1992. Published in Étienne Balibar, *La Crainte des masses. Politique et philosophie avant et après Marx* (Paris: Galilée, 1997).

2. See Jean-Claude Milner, *Les Noms indistincts* (Paris: Seuil, 1983).

3. In my books *Race, Nation, Class: Ambiguous Identities* (in collaboration with Immanuel Wallerstein) (London/New York: Verso, 1991) and *Les Frontières de la démocratie* (Paris: La Découverte, 1992).

4. The current debates on the sociology of the nation, which are in part governed by the vicissitudes of 'the construction of Europe' and the tensions that process injects into the citizenship–nationality equation, centre mainly on an examination of the differences between the French and German (or some-times British) 'models' of nationality, presenting these at times as opposing ideal types (see, for example, Dominique Schnapper's remarkable book *La France de l'intégration. Sociologie de la nation en 1990* (Paris: Gallimard, 1991)). This is, among other things, a very European way of passing over the far more decisive determination by the centre–periphery structure (which, naturally, runs through Europe itself).

5. It is, as we know, difficult *truly* to found a national society on 'hybridiza-tion' (in spite of Mexico) or on multilingualism (Switzerland and India notwith-standing); it is not clear that it is any easier to base a national society on

multi-confessionality (there is, at least, a price to pay for it, as the example of Germany shows).

6. Benedict Anderson has provided a remarkable analysis of these in his *Imagined Communities: Reflections on the Origin and Spread of Nationalism* (London: Verso, 1983).

7. There is no 'class' without a 'party', whatever the structure of that party might be. Is not feminism's problem the difficulty of determining what the anti-family (or anti-patriarchal) institution might be?

8. It is striking how the notion of 'culture' (in its dual aspect of *Kultur* and *Bildung*), after being projected on to 'peoples' without nations, enabling these to be represented as non-historical, closed 'ethnic groups', has subsequently been retro-projected on to 'national' societies, which have today entered a phase of enthusiastic self-ethnologizing.

9. It will be evident that I am, in a way, *separating* two elements which are conceived as a unity by Benedict Anderson in his description of 'Imagined Communities'. However, I am doing this in order to attempt to think their necessary articulation.

10. For the history of the symbolic transfer of the notion of 'patriotism' from the domain of religion to that of the nation-state, see Ernst Kantorowicz, '*Pro Patria Mori* in Medieval Political Thought', in *Selected Studies* (Locust Valley, NY: J. J. Augustin, 1965).

11. Ernest Gellner, 'Tractatus Sociologico-Philosophicus', in *Culture, Identity and Politics* (Cambridge: Cambridge University Press, 1987), pp. 166 ff.

12. For an attempt to interpret the history of 'real socialism' as an abortive construction of the national-social state in the 'semi-periphery', see Étienne Balibar, 'L'Europe après le communisme', in *Les Frontières de la démocratie* (Paris: La Découverte, 1992).

13. Or is distributed according to social position: those who do not have the means to be anti-American are anti-Arab, whereas many writers and academics, who would be ashamed to be anti-Arab, rail against the American 'cultural invasion'.

(*Translated by Chris Turner*)

4

What is a Border?[1]

You can be a citizen or you can be stateless, but it is difficult
to imagine *being* a border.[2]

To the question, 'What is a border?', which is certainly one of the
necessary preliminaries to our discussions, it is not possible to give
a simple answer. Why should this be? Basically, because we cannot
attribute to the border an essence which would be valid in all places
and at all times, for all physical scales and time periods, and which
would be included in the same way in all individual and collective
experience. Without going back as far as the Roman *limes*, it is clear
that the border of a European monarchy in the eighteenth century,
when the notion of cosmopolitanism was invented, has little in
common with those borders the Schengen Convention is so keen
to strengthen today. And we all know that you do not cross the
border between France and Switzerland, or between Switzerland
and Italy, the same way when you have a 'European' passport as
when you have a passport from the former Yugoslavia. It is, indeed,
to discuss such a question that we are here.

In reality, however, though it complicates matters theoretically,
the impossibility of giving a simple answer to our question is also an
opportunity. For, if we are to understand the unstable world in
which we live, we need complex notions – in other words, dialectical
notions. We might even say that we need to complicate things. And
if we are to contribute to changing this world in its unacceptable,

intolerable aspects – or (and this perhaps comes down to the same thing) to resist the changes occurring in that world, which are presented to us as inevitable – we need to overturn the false simplicity of some obvious notions.

Allow me to flirt for a minute with some of the language play of my philosopher colleagues. The idea of a simple definition of what constitutes a border is, by definition, absurd: to mark out a border is, precisely, to define a territory, to delimit it, and so to register the identity of that territory, or confer one upon it. Conversely, however, to define or identify in general is nothing other than to trace a border, to assign boundaries or borders (in Greek, *horos*; in Latin, *finis* or *terminus*; in German, *Grenze*; in French, *borne*). The theorist who attempts to define what a border is is in danger of going round in circles, as the very representation of the border is the precondition for any definition.

This point – which may seem speculative, even idle – has, none the less, a very concrete side to it. Every discussion of borders relates, precisely, to the establishment of definite identities, national or otherwise. Now, it is certain that there *are* identities – or, rather, identifications – which are, to varying degrees, active and passive, voluntary and imposed, individual and collective. Their multiplicity, their hypothetical or fictive nature, do not make them any less real. But it is obvious that these identities are not well defined. And, consequently, from a logical – or juridical or national – point of view, they are not defined at all – or, rather, they would not be if, despite the fundamental impossibility inherent in them, they were not subject to a forced definition. In other words, their practical definition requires a 'reduction of complexity', the application of a simplifying force or of what we might, paradoxically, term a supplement of simplicity. And this, naturally, also complicates many things. The state – as nation-state and as a *Rechtsstaat* – is, among other things, a formidable reducer of complexity, though its very existence is a permanent cause of complexity (we might also say of disorder), which it then falls to it to reduce.

All this, as we know, is not merely theoretical. The violent consequences are felt every day; they are constitutive of that *condition of violence*, to which the Declaration issued to launch this conference refers,[3] in the face of which we are looking for political ideas and initiatives which are not merely that 'Hobbesian' reduction of complexity which a simple central authority sanctioned by law and armed with the monopoly of legitimate violence represents – this being, in any case, an ineffectual solution at the general world level, where it could at most put down a particular troublemaker here or there. . . . In utter disregard of certain borders – or, in some cases, under cover of such borders – indefinable and impossible identities emerge in various places, identities which are, as a consequence, regarded as non-identities. However, their existence is, none the less, a life-and-death question for large numbers of human beings. This is, increasingly, a problem everywhere, and the question coming out of the horror in the 'former Yugoslavia' (the very expression speaks volumes) concerns us all in reality, and it concerns us from within, and with regard to our own history.

For borders have a history; the very notion of border has a history. And it is not the same everywhere and at every level. I shall come back to this point.[4] From our point of view, as European men and women at the very end of the twentieth century, this history seems to be moving towards an ideal of reciprocal appropriation of individuals by the state, and of the state by individuals, through the 'territory'. Or rather, as Hannah Arendt pointed out so admirably – and we are right to invoke her in this context – it is moving towards a *cusp* at which the impossibility of attaining this ideal is manifested at the very moment when it seems closest to realization. We are at that point now.

Since earliest Antiquity, since the 'origins' of the state, of city-states and empires, there have been 'borders' and 'marches' – that is to say, lines or zones, strips of land, which are places of separation and contact or confrontation, areas of blockage and passage (or passage on payment of a toll). Fixed or shifting zones, continuous or broken lines. But these borders have never had exactly the same function – not even over the last two or three centuries, despite the continuous effort of codification put in by nation-states. The 'tyranny of the national'[5] – to use Gérard Noiriel's expression – is itself constantly changing shape, including the shape of its policing. It is currently changing its functions once again, and doing so before our very eyes. One of the major implications of the Schengen Convention – which is indeed the only aspect of 'the construction of Europe' that is currently moving forward, not in the area of citizenship, but in that of *anti-citizenship*, by way of co-ordination between police forces and also of more or less simultaneous legislative and constitutional changes regarding the right of asylum and immigration regulations, family reunion, the granting of nationality, and so on – is that from now on, on 'its' border – or rather, at certain favoured *border points* of 'its' territory – each member state is becoming the representative of the others. In this way, a new mode of discrimination between the national and the alien is being established. Also changing are the conditions under which individuals *belong* to states, in the various – indissociably connected – senses of the term. One has only to see with what repugnance states, almost without exception, view dual or multiple nationality to understand how essential it is to the nation-state to behave as the owner of its nationals (and, theoretically at least, to undertake an exhaustive division of individuals between territories, with no one counted twice or left over). This is merely an adjunct to the principle of the – at least relative and symbolic – exclusion of foreigners. But there can be no doubt that, in national normality, the normality of the national citizen-subject, such an appropriation is also *internalized* by individuals, as it becomes a condition, an essential reference of their collective, communal sense, and hence, once again, of their identity (or of the order, the ranking, by which they arrange their multiple identities). As a consequence, borders cease to be purely external realities. They become also – and perhaps predominantly – what Fichte, in his *Reden an die deutsche Nation*, magnificently termed 'inner borders' [*innere Grenzen*]; that is to say – as indeed he says himself – *invisible borders*, situated everywhere and nowhere.

To attempt to understand how this operates in detail, I shall briefly touch on three major aspects of the equivocal character of borders in history. The first I shall term their *overdetermination*. The second

is their *polysemic character* – that is to say, the fact that borders never
exist in the same way for individuals belonging to different social
groups. The third aspect is their *heterogeneity* – in other words, the
fact that, in reality, several functions of demarcation and territorial-
ization – between distinct social exchanges or flows, between distinct rights, and so forth – are always fulfilled simultaneously by
borders.

1. I shall begin, then, with what I call – for the purposes of this
discussion – *overdetermination*. We know that *every border* has its own
history. Indeed, this is almost a commonplace of history textbooks.
In that history, the demand for the right to self-determination and
the power or impotence of states are combined, together with
cultural demarcations (often termed 'natural'), economic interests,
and so on. It is less often noted that no political border is ever the
mere boundary between two states, but is always *over*determined
and, in that sense, sanctioned, reduplicated and relativized by other
geopolitical divisions. This feature is by no means incidental or
contingent; it is intrinsic. Without the *world-configuring* function they
perform, there would be no borders – or no lasting borders.

Without going back beyond the modern age, let us give two
examples of this which still have effects today. The European
colonial empires – roughly from the Treaty of Tordesillas (1494) to
the 1960s – were most certainly the condition of emergence,
reinforcement and subsistence, within the framework of successive
world-economies, of the nation-states of Western – and even of
Eastern – Europe. As a result, these states' borders *with each other*
were both, indissociably, national borders and imperial borders,
with other frontiers extending and replicating them right into 'the
heart of darkness', somewhere in Africa and Asia. As a consequence,
they served to separate different categories of 'nationals'. For the
'imperial-national' states did not merely have 'citizens'; they also
had 'subjects'.[6] And those subjects, as far as the national administration was concerned, were both *less foreign than aliens*, and yet *more
different (or more 'alien') than them*: which means that in some respects,

or in some circumstances (as in times of war), it was sometimes easier for them to cross borders than it was for aliens in the strict sense, and sometimes more difficult.

A second example is that of the 'camps' or blocs in the Cold War between 1945 and 1990. Whereas the 'division of the world' between colonial empires *strengthens* national sovereignty in some cases (while purely and simply preventing it in others), the division into blocs (to which, we should not forget, the creation and operation of the UN was a corollary) seems to have combined an extension of the nation-form worldwide (and, consequently, of an – at least theoretical – *national identity* as the 'basic' identity for all individuals) with the creation of a *de facto* hierarchy among those nations within each bloc, and, as a result, more or less limited sovereignty for most of them. This meant that the national borders of states were once again overdetermined and, depending on the particular case, strengthened or weakened. It also meant that there were once again, in practice, several types of aliens and alienness, and several different modes of border-crossing. When the border, or the sense of crossing a border, coincided with the super-borders of the blocs, it was generally more difficult to pass through, because the alien in this case was also an enemy alien, if not indeed a potential spy. This was the case *except* where refugees were concerned, because the right of asylum was used as a weapon in the ideological struggle. Might it not be said that the dispositions for asylum seekers which passed into law in the 1950s and 1960s, both in international conventions and national constitutions, owe much of their formulation and their theoretical liberalism to this situation? The German law, which has just been changed, is an – extreme – example which illustrates this very clearly.

If we did not keep this situation in mind, it seems to me that we would not understand the terms in which the question of refugees from Eastern Europe currently presents itself (from that Eastern Europe which is suddenly no longer Eastern Europe any more, but almost a part of the Third World).[7] Nor would we understand the difficulties the 'European Community' has in seeing itself *as a community* underpinned by specific interests of its own, whereas it was essentially the by-product, and part of the mechanism, of the

Cold War – even in so far as the aim of constituting a counterweight to American hegemonic power within the 'Western bloc' was concerned.

The colonial empires of the past and the 'blocs' of the recent past have left deep marks on institutions, law and mentalities. But they no longer exist. It would, however, be naive to think that they have now given way to a mere juxtaposition of similar nations. What is today termed the crisis of the nation-state is partly (even if it is not *only*) the objective uncertainty regarding, on the one hand, the nature and location of the geopolitical demarcations which may overdetermine borders and, on the other, what type or degree of national autonomy these hypothetical super-borders might be compatible with, given their military, economic, ideological or symbolic operation. With the question of the inner (ethnic, social or religious) divisions within each nation-state – and even within very 'ancient' ones – it might well be that this tormenting but generally unacknowledged question, fraught with potential conflict, will be decisive in determining *which national borders* in Europe itself are likely to survive into the new historical period. The borders of Germany have already changed; those of Yugoslavia and Czechoslovakia, too, by two very different processes. It could be that others further West will follow.

2. Second, I come to what I have referred to, in a perhaps rather overblown fashion, as the *polysemic nature* of borders. In practical terms, this simply refers to the fact that they do not have the same meaning for everyone. The facts of this are commonly known, and indeed, form the core of our discussion here. Nothing is less like a material thing than a border, even though it is officially 'the same' (identical to itself, and therefore well defined) whichever way you cross it – whether you do so as a businessman or an academic travelling to a conference, or as a young unemployed person. In this latter case, a border becomes almost two distinct entities, which have nothing in common but a *name*. Today's borders (though in reality this has long been the case) are, to some extent, designed to perform precisely this task: not merely to give individuals from different social classes different experiences of the law, the civil

administration, the police and elementary rights, such as the freedom of circulation and freedom of entreprise, but actively to *differentiate* between individuals in terms of social class.

Here the state, settled on and constituted by its own borders, has, over the course of history, played a fundamentally ambivalent role, for on the one side it conceals – and, up to a point, formally limits – differentiation, in order to insist upon the notion of national citizen and, through that notion, a certain primacy of the public authority over social antagonisms. On the other hand, however, the more transnational traffic – whether of people or of capital – intensifies, the more a transnational politico-economic space has formed as a result, and the more states – including, particularly, the most 'powerful' among them – tend to operate in the service of an international class differentiation, and, to that end, to use their borders and apparatuses of control as instruments of discrimination and triage. Yet they attempt to do this while preserving to the utmost the symbolic sources of their popular legitimacy. This is why they find themselves in the contradictory position of having both to relativize *and* to reinforce the notion of identity and national belonging, the equation of citizenship with nationality.

There is a double-bind of the same kind inherent in the very notion of the circulation of persons. The problem lies not so much in the difference in treatment between the circulation of commodities or capital and the circulation of people, as the term circulation is not used here in the same sense. It is, rather, the fact that, in spite of computer networks and telecommunications, capital never circulates without a plentiful circulation of human beings – some circulating 'upwards', others 'downwards'. But the establishment of a world *apartheid*, or a dual regime for the circulation of individuals, raises massive political problems of acceptability and resistance. The 'colour bar', which no longer now merely separates 'centre' from 'periphery', or North from South, but runs through *all* societies, is for this very reason an uneasy approximation to such an apartheid. The actual management of this 'colour bar' has a massive but double-edged impact, because it reinforces an uncontrollable racism, and promotes insecurity – and this in turn necessitates an excessive degree of security provision. Not to mention the fact that between the two extremes – between those who 'circulate capital' and those 'whom capital circulates', through 'transnational relocations' of industrial plant and 'flexibility', there is an enormous, unclassifiable, intermediate mass.

It is perhaps also from this point of view that we should reflect on one of the most odious aspects of the question of refugees and migration, to which Marie-Claire Caloz-Tschopp and her friends have recently devoted a detailed study: the question of 'international zones' or 'transit zones' in ports and airports.[8] Not only do we have here an illustration of the state of generalized violence which now forms the backdrop both to so-called economic migration and to the flows of refugees, recognized or unrecognized, but we see here in material reality the differential operation and, so to speak, duplication of the notion of border which was already beginning to emerge in the different formalities which applied to the crossing of borders.

We must not confine ourselves solely to a discussion of the legal aspects here; it is essential that we also undertake a phenomenological description. For a rich person from a rich country, a person who tends towards the cosmopolitan (and whose passport increasingly *signifies* not just mere national belonging, protection and a right of citizenship, but a *surplus* of rights – in particular, a world right to circulate unhindered), the border has become an embarkation formality, a point of symbolic acknowledgement of his social status, to be passed at a jog-trot. For a poor person from a poor country, however, the border tends to be something quite different: not only is it an obstacle which is very difficult to surmount, but it is a place he runs up against repeatedly, passing and repassing through it as and when he is expelled or allowed to rejoin his family, so that it becomes, in the end, a place where he *resides*. It is an extraordinarily viscous spatio-temporal zone, almost a home – a home in which to live a life which is a waiting-to-live, a non-life. The psychoanalyst André Green once wrote that it is difficult enough to live *on* a border, but that is as nothing compared with *being* a border oneself. He meant this in the sense of the splitting of multiple identities – migrant identities – but we must also look at the material bases of the phenomenon.

3. This would lead me quite naturally, if I had the time, to discuss my third point: the heterogeneity and ubiquity of borders or, in other words, the fact that the tendency of borders, political, cultural and socioeconomic, to _coincide_ – something which was more or less well achieved by nation-states, or, rather, by some of them – is tending today to fall apart. The result of this is that *some borders are no longer situated at the borders at all*, in the geographico-politico-administrative sense of the term. They are in fact elsewhere, wherever selective controls are to be found, such as, for example, *health* or *security* checks (health checks being part of what Michel Foucault termed bio-power). The concentration of all these functions (for example, the control of goods and people – not to mention microbes and viruses – administrative and cultural separation, etc.) at a single point – along a single line which was simultaneously refined and densified, opacified – was a dominant tendency during a particular period, the period of the nation-state (when it really existed in a form close to its ideal type), but not an irreversible historical necessity. For quite some time now, it has been giving way, before our very eyes, to a new ubiquity of borders.

What I wanted to stress – perhaps it is a truism – is that in the historical complexity of the notion of border – which is currently becoming important for us again, just as it is changing and assuming new forms – there is the question of the *institution*. The institution of the border, of course, and the ways in which borders can be instituted, but also there is the border as a condition of possibility of a whole host of institutions. If the border was defined fictively in a simple, simplistic way and if, as I suggested at the beginning, that simplicity was *forced* – that is to say, subjected to forcing by the state – it was precisely for this reason. But the consequence has been that the borders within which the conditions for a relative democracy have in some cases been won have themselves always been absolutely anti-democratic institutions, beyond the reach of any political purchase or practice. 'Citizens' have settled there for any length of time only for purposes of mutual extermination. . . .

Borders have been the anti-democratic condition for that partial, limited democracy which some nation-states enjoyed for a certain period, managing their own internal conflicts (sometimes *exporting* them too, but that is very much a process which requires a border line). This is why I think you are right in your Declaration to speak of a requirement for 'radical democracy'. As soon as borders become differentiated and multiple once again – once they begin to constitute a *grid* ranging over the new social space, and cease simply to border it from the outside – then the alternative lies between an authoritarian, and indeed violent, intensification of all forms of segregation, and a democratic radicalism which has as its aim to deconstruct the institution of the border.

For my own part, however, I would hesitate to identify such a radical democracy – which is necessarily internationalist or, more accurately, transnational – with the pursuit of a 'borderless world' in the juridico-political sense of the term. Such a 'world' would run the risk of being a mere arena for the unfettered domination of the private centres of power which monopolize capital, communications and, perhaps also, arms. It is a question, rather, of what democratic control is to be exerted on the controllers of borders – that is to say, on states and supra-national institutions themselves. This depends entirely on whether those on the different sides of the border eventually discover common interests and a common language (common ideals). But it depends also on the question of *who* will meet in those unliveable places that are the different borders. Now, in order to meet, one most often needs interpreters, mediators. Disheartening as their experience is today, it seems to me that those who defend the right of asylum precisely rank among those mediators.

Notes

1. Paper delivered to the conference, 'Violence et droit d'asile en Europe: Des frontières des États-Nations à la responsabilité partagée dans un seul monde', organized by Marie-Claire Caloz-Tschopp and Axel Clévenot, University of Geneva, 23–25 September 1993. Published in Étienne Balibar, *La Crainte des masses. Politique et et philosophie avant et après Marx* (Paris: Galilée, 1997).

2. André Green, *La Folie privée. Psychanalyse des cas-limites* (Paris: Gallimard, 1990), p. 107.

3. 'Violence is a *condition of existence* in societies of exile and in the societies of the north': Founding Declaration of the conference 'Violence et droit d'asile en Europe', reprinted in Marie-Claire Caloz-Tschopp, Axel Clévenot and Maria-Pia Tschopp (eds), *Asile – Violence – Exclusion en Europe. Histoire, analyse, prospective* (Geneva: Cahiers de la Section des Sciences de l'Éducation de l'Université de Genève/ Groupe de Genève 'Violence et droit d'Asile en Europe', 1994).

4. This history, together with an anthropology and a semantics of borders, is beginning to be written. See D. Nordmann, 'Des limites d'État aux frontières nationales', in P. Nora (ed.), *Les Lieux de mémoire*, vol. II (Paris: Gallimard, 1986) p. 35 ff; P. Sahlins, *Boundaries: The Making of France and Spain in the Pyrenees* (Berkeley, University of California Press, 1989); M. Foucher, *Fronts et frontières* (Paris: Fayard, 1991); and the Autumn 1995 number of *Quaderni*, ed. Yves Winkin, on the theme 'Penser la frontière'.

5. See Gérard Noiriel, *La Tyrannie du national* (Paris: Calmann-Lévy, 1991).

6. See Étienne Balibar, 'Sujets ou citoyens – Pour l'égalité' in, *Les frontières de la démocratie* (Paris: La Découverte, 1992).

7. Balibar writes: 'cet Est qui soudain n'est plus l'Est mais plutôt une sorte de demi-Sud' I have adapted this from the French cultural context in which *l'Est* is Eastern Europe and *le Sud* the source of most 'Third-World' immigration. [Trans.]

8. Marie-Claire Caloz-Tschopp (ed.), *Frontières du droit, frontières des droits. L'introuvable statut de la 'zone internationale'* (Paris: L'Harmattan, 1993),

(Translated by Chris Turner)

5

The Borders of Europe

The 'borders of Europe': does the 'of' indicate an objective or a subjective genitive? As we shall see, both are necessarily involved, and what is at stake is precisely the 'Europeanness' of Europe's borders.

A reflection on the borders of Europe might well be the least abstract way at our disposal of leaving behind a continualy ruminated philosopheme which has been given renewed youth by the proliferation of discussions about the future, the meaning, the culture, and the cultural exceptionalism of Europe: namely, the antithesis of the particular and the universal. But it might also be, more speculatively, a way of understanding how a certain conception of the universal and the particular as opposites has imposed itself among those who want or believe themselves to be 'Europeans', a conception that has assigned philosophy the task – its highest task, even – of sublating the abstraction of this opposition in a superior 'synthesis'. The figure of the unity of opposites (which is itself in many ways subtended by the schema or metaphor of the border) has never abolished this conception. On the contrary, it has confirmed that what can be *demarcated*, *defined*, and *determined* maintains a constitutive relation with what can be *thought*. Putting into question the notion of the border – indissociably 'concept' and 'image,' or, rather, prior to the very distinction (must we call it 'European'?) between concept and image – thus always in some sense implies a confrontation with the impossible limit of an autodetermination, a *Selbstbestimmung* of thought. It implies an effort to conceptualize the line *on which we think*, the condition of possibility or the 'hidden art' of distributions and delimitations.

One might wonder why this task should be any easier today than it was in the past. Indeed, it may not be. But it is all the more inescapable in so far as we are living in a conjuncture of the vacillation of borders – both their layout and their function – that is at the same time a vacillation of the very notion of border, which has become particularly equivocal. This vacillation affects our very consciousness of a European 'identity', because Europe is the point in the world whence border lines set forth to be drawn throughout the world, because it is the native land of the very representation of the border as this sensible and supersensible 'thing' that should be or not be, be here or there, a bit beyond [*jenseits*] or short of [*diesseits*] its ideal 'position', but always somewhere.[1]

This observation of an uncertainty in the representation of borders is not contradicted by the insistence (which can be violent or peaceful) on the unsurpassable or sacred character of borders, and may even explain it.[2] The conjuncture in which we are currently living in Europe – from the Atlantic to the Urals, unless it be to the Amur River; from the Nordkapp to the Bosphorus, unless it be to the Persian Gulf: wherever the representation of the border as particularization and partition of the universal reigns – is producing a brutal short cicuit of the 'empirical' and 'transcendental' dimensions of the notion of the border. This conjuncture immediately makes questions of administration and diplomacy, politics and policing, into philosophical questions. It confers a practical import on speculative decisions about the meaning of defining an 'interior' and an 'exterior', a 'here' and a 'there', and generally about everything that Kant would have called the amphibologies of reflection.

In such a conjuncture, it is necessary to try to think what it is difficult even to imagine. But it can also be fruitful to work on the imagination itself, to explore its possibilities of variation. In *La Folie privée*, André Green notes: 'You can be a citizen or you can be stateless, but it is difficult to imagine *being* a border.'[3] But isn't this

precisely what, all around us, many individuals, groups and territories must indeed try to imagine? It is precisely what they are
living, what most intimately affects their 'being' in so far as it is
neither this nor that. This is perhaps what all of Europe, and not just
its 'margins', 'marches' or 'outskirts', must imagine today, for it has
become a daily experience. Most of the areas, nations and regions
that constitute Europe had become accustomed to thinking that
they had borders, more or less 'secure and recognized', but they
did not think they *were* borders.

I will sketch out this variation around three aspects of the
problem (in a sense the 'real', the 'symbolic', and the 'imaginary'
of the border): (1) the current vacillation of borders; (2) the
interiority and ideality of borders; and (3) the conflict or the
overlapping of 'cultures' around what – going back to an old
archetype – I will call the European *triple point*.

The Vacillation of Borders

The fact that borders are vacillating is a matter of experience: first
and foremost, they are no longer *at the border*, an institutional site
that can be materialized on the ground and inscribed on the map,
where one sovereignty *ends* and another *begins*; where individuals
(ex)change obligations as well as currency; where in peacetime
Customs examinations, verifications of identity, and payment of
duties and tolls are carried out; where in wartime armed populations converge, coming to defend the *Fatherland* by attacking the
enemy's *expansionism*. I will not discuss here the question of
whether this institutional form of the border is ancient or recent,
universal or particular. I shall recall, rather, that it is the result of a
long gestation, of a series of *choices* none of which was necessary,
but choices that led to one another, and coincide with the universalization of a very particular form of state, originating in Europe:
the *nation*-state. And I shall simply observe that this institution,
today, is irreversibly coming undone.

With respect to the question that concerns us, this situation did not begin when the Maastricht Treaty came into effect, nor with the announced application of the Schengen Convention. The malady 'comes from further afield'.[4]

It comes from the transformation of the means of international communication, which has relativized the functions of the *port of entry* and, by contrast, revalorized internal controls, creating within each territory *zones of transit* and transition, populations 'awaiting' entry or exit (sometimes for several years, sometimes in a periodically repeated fashion), individually or collectively engaged in a process of *negotiation* of their presence and their mode of presence (that is, their political, economic, cultural, religious, and other rights) with one or more states.[5]

It comes from the fact that the speed of purchase and sale orders and monetary conversion, executed in 'real time' (even integrating 'rational anticipations' of the behaviour of public and private agents into the computer's imaginary), has gone far beyond the possibilities of control on the part of administrations (to say nothing of control on the part of citizens).

It comes from the fact that the appropriaton of 'natural' (or natural-cultural) factors 'common to the human race' by individuals or groups themselves controlled and appropriated by states has encountered its limits. The cloud generated by Chernobyl cannot be stopped at the border, nor can the AIDS virus, despite the reinforced control that some dream of imposing on its 'carriers', which means on virtually all of us. Nor can one stop CNN's images, even by regulating the sale of satellite dishes. At most one can try to superimpose other images on them by jamming signals on a worldwide scale.

It comes from the fact that the methods of modern warfare no longer *cross* borders in the strict sense (let us recall such archaeological formulas and images as the 'violation of Belgian neutrality' and tanks knocking over boundary posts), but virtually (and actually, as the Gulf War proved) overhang them, that is, negate them.

It comes from the fact that the class struggle, as we used to say (or, as we would say today, the managing of phenomena of inequality and exclusion, and of the flows of active and inactive populations), has definitively escaped the jurisdiction of nation-states, without thereby coming under the control of apparatuses that could be called 'global'.

It comes from the fact that there has occurred a tendential inversion of power relations in the hierarchy of idioms in which the formation of individuals and the cultural recognition of groups, and consequently the very evolution of languages, are carried out. (This hierarchy has *always* combined the three levels of the national, the dialectal – or 'vernacular', whether socially or regionally defined – and the transnational – easily baptized the 'universal'.)[6]

It comes from the fact that the possibility of *concentrating* in a single place ('capital', 'metropolis') the exercise of political power, economic decision-making, and the production of aesthetic models has definitively disappeared.

And, to conclude, it comes from the fact that the response by some European nations – or rather, by their ruling classes – to these different processes of '*globalization*' has been to initiate a transfer of institutions to the supra-national level, a process whose very signification (the juridico-political status and the value that it confers on the idea of 'community') continues, and probably will continue, to *divide them on the question of union* for an unforeseeable time to come.

Thus borders are vacillating. This means that they are no longer localizable in an unequivocal fashion. It also means that they no longer allow a superimposition of the set of functions of sovereignty, administration, cultural control, taxation, and so on, and consequently a conferral on the territory or, better, on the duo of territory and population – of a simultaneously englobing and univocal signification of 'presupposition' for all other social relations.[7] Moreover, it means that they do not work in the same way for 'things' and 'people' – not to mention what is *neither thing nor person*: viruses, information, ideas – and thus repeatedly pose, sometimes in a violent way, the question of whether people transport, send, and receive things, or whether things transport, send, and receive people: what can in general be called the empirico-transcendental question of *luggage*. Finally, it means that they do not work *in the same way*, 'equally', for all 'people', and notably not for those who come from different parts of the world, who (this is more or less the same thing) do not have the same social status, the same relation to the appropriation and exchange of idioms.[8] This properly *social* differentiation is already in the course of powerfully disaggregating the modern equation – whose identitarian logic is fundamentally based on the concept of the border[9] – of *citizenship* and *nationality*, and consequently or irreversibly transforming the very notion of people, *peuple, Volk, narod, umran,* and *aςabiyya,* and so on, for this equation presupposes that we can maintain at least as a legal fiction (but all law is fictive, or fictional), the equality of citizenships as an equality of nationalities.[10]

Borders are vacillating. This does not mean that they are disappering. Less then ever is the contemporary world a 'world without borders'. On the contrary, borders are being both multiplied and reduced in their localization and their function; they are being thinned out and doubled, becoming borders *zones, regions,* or *countries* where one can reside and live. The quantitative relation between 'border' and 'territory' is being inverted. This means that borders are becoming the object of protest and contestation as well as of an unremitting reinforcement, notably of their security function. But this also means – irreversibly – that borders have stopped marking the limits where politics ends because the community ends (whether the community is conceived of in terms of 'contract' or 'origin' has only a relative importance here, to tell the truth, because the practical result is the same), beyond which, in Clausewitz's words, politics can be continued only 'by other means'. This in fact means that borders are no longer the shores of the political, but have indeed become – perhaps by way of the police, given that every border patrol is today an organ of 'internal security' – *objects* or – let us put it more precisely – *things* within the space of the political itself.

The Interiority and Ideality of Borders

This situation allows us to return to the border's past, and to correct a representation that seems natural, but is none the less manifestly false, or in any case too simple: the representation that makes the border the simple limit between two territorial entities, similar to but independent of one another. Contemporary globalization is certainly bringing about what can be called an *under*determination of the border, a weakening of its identity. But the border is no less troubled by the recent memory, the insistent afterimage of the inverse figure: that of the *over*determination of borders. By this I mean to designate the fact that, *at least in Europe* (but this model is one that 'we' have proposed to and imposed upon the entire world, through conquest and colonization, then decolonization and the establishment of the 'league of nations'), state borders, understood equally as the borders of a culture and an at-least-*fictive* identity, have always been immediately endowed with a *global* signification. They have always served not only to separate particularities, but always also at the same time, *in order to* fulfil this 'local' function, to 'partition the world', *to configure* it, to give it a representable figure in the modality of the partition, distribution and attribution of regions of space, or – to put it better – of the *historical* distribution of the regions of space, which would work like the instantaneous projection of the progresses and processes of its history. Every *map* in this sense is always a world map, for it represents a 'part of the world', it locally projects the *universitas* that is *omnitudo compartium absoluta*.[11]

We would need time here to illustrate this thesis by a series of examples, to linger on the succession of figures of the symbolic overdetermination of borders, which is present here as the immediately global import of the slightest bend of a border. We would have to enumerate all its theologico-political names, from the first division of the world made by Pope Alexander VI between the Spanish and the Portuguese at the Treaty of Tordesillas (1494),[12] immediately contested by others (the English, the French), up to its modern equivalents: the division of Africa at the Conference of Berlin (1895), or the division of Yalta. We would have to show – this time taking up the anlyses of Braudel and Wallerstein – how the division of the world between Europeans or quasi-Europeans has always been the condition of the (at least relative) *stabilization* of the borders which, in Europe itself, separated states from one another, and constituted the condition of their 'equilibrium'. And we would have to notice the same figure everywhere: that of a *binary* division of world space (of the 'sphere' or the whole) that is disturbed not so much by the fluctuations of the balance of power between 'blocs' as by the intervention of a *third*, which can be manifested as aggression, resistance, or even a simple 'passive' presence that renders the partition invalid. We would then have to write the history of the successive 'Third Worlds' – even before the invention of the expression – and see how, each time, they blurred the local question of the partition of the world because, ideologically as much as strategically, they blurred the representation of the globe. But above all, we would have to show that such an overdetermination is never – however decisive this aspect may be – a simple question of external power, of relations of force and the distrubition of populations between states, but always *also*, as Derrida has correctly emphasized, a question of idealities: a 'spiritual' question, therefore – or, better still, a symbolic question.

National borders would not be capable of securing (or trying to secure) *identities*, would not be capable of marking the threshold at which life and death are played out (in what in Europe is called 'patriotism');[13] in brief – to take up the decisive formulation elaborated by Fichte in the *Addresses to the German Nation* (1807) – they would not be capable of being 'internal borders' (internalized borders, borders for interiority) were they not idealized. And they would not be idealized, conceived of as the support of the universal, if they were not imagined as the point at which 'world-views' [*Weltanschauungen, conceptions du monde*], and thus also views of man, were at stake: the point at which one must choose, and choose *oneself*.

But the term *world-view* is much too vague – or, more precisely, it is frighteningly equivocal. For it can cover, as need be, the notion of *cultural difference* (whether it be a question of rituals, manners, or traditions): a fundamentally *imaginary* notion, since the principle of its definition is the perception of 'similarities' and 'dissimilarities', the principle of proximity and distance. Or it can cover the notion of *symbolic difference*, for which, in order to make myself understood, I will reserve the name of a difference in civilization: a difference that bears not upon resemblance but upon the reconcilable and the irreconcilable, the compatible and the incompatible.

Everyone can feel, to take only one example from contemporary situations, that when the French (although certainly not all of them) indignantly decry the sentencing of two children found guilty of murder to 'detention at Her Majesty's pleasure' – it being by no means certain that this sentence is unanimously approved by the English – at the exact moment that their own Minister of Justice presents himself as the spokesman for a public opinion demanding a 'genuine life sentence' for murderers and rapists of children,[14] it is not a cultural difference that is at play, but a symbolic trait, or a trait of civilization, that bears upon the way in which 'subjects' relate themselves to childhood and adulthood, innocence and perversion, the relation between 'act' and 'intention', 'responsibility' and 'irresponsibility' in the definition of crime. Everyone can thus understand that such differences have little or nothing to do with 'cultural distance', or rather, that they are probably all the more marked where the cultural proximity is greatest, and thus that it is much more difficult to imagine a harmonizing of the French and English (or Anglo-American and Franco-German) judicial systems than to resolve the question of the acceptance or rejection of the so-called Islamic veils worn by some young women in the schools of the French Republic. I will even risk the hypothesis that in this respect each fraction of Europe, however, restricted it may be, still contains, actually or potentially, as the result of history and the subjective choices it has occasioned, the same diversity and divisions as the world considered in its totality.

Traditionally, the disciplines of history and sociology have assigned the differential traits of civilization, in this sense, to the domain of the *religious*. This is no doubt a consequence of the properly European identification of the general notion of the symbolic with religious idealities – in other words, of the fact that the master-signifiers in whose name the interpellation of individuals as subjects occurs in Europe or, more precisely, in the Mediterranean basin – are religious words, or words with a religious background. 'Patriotism' and 'law' are good examples. It is thus also a

consequence of the fact that the establishment (and later crisis) of
secular state hegemonies, whose form of universality is above all
juridico-political, does not simply take over in a linear way from the
establishment and crisis of religious hegemonies or universalisms.
The crisis of the nation-state has begun in today's Europe, without
any foreseeable end, whereas the crisis of reglious consciousness is
by no means completed or resolved. The same precautions are
necessary, however, with respect to the notion of 'religion' as that
of 'border': no one knows what religion in general is; or rather, no
one can define the difference between a religious symbol and a
profane symbol other than by a tautological reference to what has
gradually been identified as 'religion' in the history of Europe. And
everywhere that history has been rethought on the European
model.

The Conflict or Overlapping of Cultures around the
European Triple Point

Let us nevertheless admit an identification of the religious and the
symbolic, at least as a provisional working hypothesis. We will then
see the symbolic overdetermination of borders in a new light. We
can reformulate a number of our observations – that borders are
always double; that they can separate particular territories only by
structuring the universality of the world; and that this doubling is
the very condition of their internalization by individuals, and thus
of their function as constitutive of identities – by saying that every
instituted, demanded, or fantasized border must be both a political
border and a religious border in this sense. And, conversely, we can
say that the only way to realize the border as an absolute separation
is to represent it as a religious border – even when this religion is a
lay, secularized religion, a religion of language, school, and constitutional principle.[15]

I believe that an idea of this sort is at work, for example, in Rémi
Brague's book *Europe, la voie romaine* – one of the few that might
survive the current overproduction of historico-philosophical works
on the theme of 'European identity'.[16] Brague seeks the definition

of European identity in an interplay of splits, successive religious demarcations, which he sees as having fractured the proto-European, circum-Mediterranean space between Antiquity and our time: Orient and Occident, North and South, with each of these axes being capable of reduplicating itself one or more times. The 'definition' of Europeanness that he arrives at is of the greatest interest. In many respects it revives, across other teleologies, the Hegelian concept of *historicity* – that is, the conflictual movement that projects each 'principle' of civilization outside of itself, towards a sublation that will call for its own sublation, and so on. This definition characterizes Roman-Latin-European identity neither by an *origin*, nor a *foundation*, nor a fidelity to authentic *roots* that would be proper to it, but by *tradition* itself: the betrayal and transmission of a heritage (which supposes its betrayal), which he calls 'belatedness' [*secondarité*]. Europeans, according to Brague, are, strictly speaking, neither 'Jews' nor 'Greeks' (the great dilemma that inflamed the nineteenth century from Renan to Matthew Arnold), but still and always 'Romans', because they *inherit* from the Greeks and the Jews (or the Semites) a logos which is not their own, and which as a consequence they can appropriate only on the condition of endlessly transforming it and transmitting it again – which, we know, can mean imposing it – beyond every pre-established border. At the limit, we can say: on the condition of *losing* it.

tradition

Nevertheless, Brague manifestly *believes* in 'Latinity' or 'Romanity' understood in this sense, and he believes in it for reasons that are as much properly religious as 'cultural'. For him, the centre of the *orbis* is indeed in the *urbs*, and more precisely in the Loggia of Saint Peter's Square, whence shines forth the splendour of truth [*splendor veritatis*]. This is why, having defined identity in terms of a *structural* schema, which as such is formal or differential (a fact expressed by the perfectly universalizable notion of 'belatedness', a phenomenon whose best contemporary examples are no doubt given by North America and even more by Japan, the double inheritor of the foreign civilizations of China and the Occident), he none the less ends up considering the structure of transmission and betrayal as specifically attached to a site, to a space – in brief, as having its historico-natural site *on one side* rather than the other of the split

between Orient and Occident (namely, in the West), *on one side* of
the split between North and South (or Christianity and Islam),
namely, on the northern, 'Christian shore' of the Mediterranean.
For him as for so many others, the thought of structure ends up
repeating a thought of substance.

It does not seem to me that we can escape the constraints of this
sort of repetition without difficulty. But personally, I prefer to work
directly with another schema of the configuration of the world,
which, moreover, seems to me to be subjacent to Brague's own
argument. I call this schema the *triple point*,[17] or *triple point of heresy*
(in the etymological sense of *heresy*, which is also the foundation of
its theological, or theologico-political, sense: to *choose* one side
rather than the other in the symbolic order, and thus to represent
error as truth and truth as error). I do not have time here to give
its full genealogy.[18] We should still recall that this figure is constitutive of the very representation of Europe as a 'part of the world'
comparable to Africa (or Libya) and Asia. It is thus at the origin of
a cartography that engendered the very notion of the border, in its
different uses. It begins with the inscription of the letter *tau* within
a circle ('schema T/O') that the Greeks, and notably Herodotus,
opposed to the figure of earth and ocean as concentric circles, and
in which the Christians later believed that they *saw* Christ's cross, as
if inscribed in a predestined way upon the very face of the earth.[19]
It is still to be found in the great Romantic myth of the 'European
Triarchy', as displayed in the title of Moses Hess's book (1841),
which in Marxism will become the interpretative schema of the
'three sources' (economics, politics, philosophy: England, France,
Germany). One can find in it one of the privileged figures of the
mirroring by which the figure of the world can be found in the
constitution of Europe, in such a way that the universality of the
world exhibits in return, at every moment, its essential Europeanness. One finds it again, to be sure, in the three empires of Orwell's
1984, which today many imagine as the United States, Western
Europe, and Japan (or China).

I am proposing only a slight variation on this traditional figure.
(Even more than traditional, it is archetypal, and in that sense
imprescriptible, but not necessarily inalterable, for its contours and

its point of application can shift.) But I believe that this variation is sufficient to put the representation of borders back in motion. I propose that Europe is not, and never has been, made up of separate regions ('empires', 'blocs', 'nations'), but, rather, of over-lapping sheets of layers [*de nappes qui se recouvrent*], and that its *overlap* specificity is this overlapping itself: to be precise, an East, a West, and a South. This was already the case in Herodotus' time, and it is not necessary to subscribe to all of Martin Bernal's hypothesis[20] in order to suppose that the triple point constituted by the meeting of the Mediterranean, the Nile, and the Tanaïs (the Don) is much more a zone of interpenetration of 'Germanic', 'Semitic' and 'Egyptian' (or 'Libyan') cultures than a line of segregation. This is even more so the case today, when – European nations having conquered the world, and then having had to officially withdraw, but without burning their bridges – it is *from the whole world* that the discourse, capitals, labour-powers, and sometimes the weapons of Europe come back to us, as a backlash.

I see advantages to working and playing with representations of this sort, rather than allowing them to act on us unperceived, outside our consciousness and our grasp. The primary advantage is to alert us to the significations that are at work in every tracing of a border, beyond the immediate, apparently factual determinations of language, religion, ideology, and power relations. One cannot but feel that it is an idea, an image, and a fantasy of Europe that, before our very eyes, are producing their deadly effects in the 'partition' and 'ethnic cleansing' of Yugoslavia generally and of Bosnia in particular, and that Europe is in the course of committing suicide by allowing the suicide in its name of these fragments of a single 'people', whose whole history is constituted by the repercussions of its own divisions.

But it is necessary to say more: 'Croats', 'Serbs' and 'Muslims' are definitely neither nations nor religions. Unfortunately for them, they are much more – voluntary or involuntary incarnations of 'irreconcilable' civilizations – and also much less – simple clan solidarities, reappearing as the ultimate recourse against the ravaging of the political identities of 'modernity'. In reality, I see only one name that is fully appropriate to them: *they are races.* By this we should understand reciprocal racisms, as 'Semites' and 'Aryans' were 'races' in Europe. Yugoslavia is a 'triple point' of European racial relations. As a consequence, what is being played out there, before us and by us, is the question of whether a state, a nation, a democracy, a society, is contructed by the dissociation or by the combination, the overlapping, of the components of every 'European' culture, on the scale of the continent as on the scale of each of its parts, its local projections.

But what can be read, as a far-off trace and as a current dilemma, in greater Europe or in each little Europe, can now also be found in many other parts of the world. This is why I will suggest that today, around the world, there are many other Europes that we do not know how to recognize. We are always narcissistically in search of images of ourselves, when it is structures that we should be looking for. Ever since the dichotomy of the two blocs, which collapsed because of its very success, was officially abolished, triple points have been reappearing everywhere: Easts, Souths, Wests. To put it plainly, these are the cultural or identitarian overlappings in which the possibility of constructing political singularities is played out today. Each of these figures has its own history and its own dynamic, but all of them are constituted by working on European schemas of partition and the border, and adapting them to their own contingencies.

This is why they all teach us that Europe is everywhere outside of itself, and that in this sense there is no more Europe – or that there will be less and less of it. But, in this dissemination without recourse, there is never more to be lost than there is to be gained – not in terms of the essence or substance of Europe, but in terms of the capacity of thinking and the project of governing oneself that it also represented.

Notes

This essay was first presented at the conference 'L'idée de l'Europe et la philosophie', sponsored by the Association des professeurs de philosophie de l'académie de Poitiers, in Poitiers, France, 2–4 December 1993. An amended and expanded version was published in Étienne Balibar, *La Crainte des masses. Politique et philosophie avant et après Marx* (Paris: Galilée, 1997).

1. Here again, there would be occasion to undertake a reflection of thought upon itself, and to pose the question of the intimate relation between the representation of the border, often the site where life and death are played out, and the idea of a unique 'passage' between 'life' and 'death', the 'other of life' and the 'other life', which has determined all 'European' theology and ethics – with the proviso that it was the Egyptians who first thought it under the form that we have inherited. See Yvette Conry,' Frontières de vie, frontières de mort', *Raison présente*, 85 (1988), pp. 49–70.

2. 'The rehabilitation of the border is today the condition of any politics, as it is the condition of any true exchange.' Philippe Séguin, 'La république et l'exception française', *Philosophie politique*, 4 (1993), pp. 45–62. [Séguin was at the time the president of the French National Assembly. – Trans.]

3. André Green, *La Folie privée: Psychanalyse des cas-limites* (Paris: Gallimard, 1990), p. 107.

4. [See Racine's *Phèdre*, Act 1, scene 3: 'Mon mal vient de plus loin.' – Trans.]

5. See, on this point, the volume edited by Marie-Claire Caloz-Tschopp (with a preface by François Julien Laferrière), *Frontières du droit, frontières des droits: L'introuvable status de la 'zone internationale'* (Paris: L'Harmattan/ANAFE, 1993).

6. For the complete history of the decisive event in the representation of universalism and particularism in the element of language – that is, the proclamation by the Academy of Berlin in 1784 of the 'universality of the French language' – see Ferdinand Brunot, *Histoire de la langue française* (Paris: Librairie Armand Colin, 1935), vol. VII.

7. This is what Gilles Deleuze and Félix Guattari described not long ago in *A Thousand Plateaus: Capitalism and Schizophrenia*, trans. Brian Massumi (Minneapolis: University of Minnesota Press, 1987), in a half-realist, half-fantastical way, as the entry into the era of 'deterritorialized flows', a new era of 'nomadism', which can be a nomadism *on the spot*.

8. If I may be permitted a personal memory here, I first became conscious of this question the day when, after we had shared beer and chocolate, an old Indian fisherman from the shores of lake Pátzcuaró (state of Michaocán, Mexico) explained to me in perfect Spanish (by which I mean Spanish that I understand without difficulty) that he had finally figured out why his attempts to emigrate to the United States had always failed: because, he told me, 'there is a letter missing' in Tarasca (his maternal language); 'hace falta una letra, entiendes amigo'. This letter, lost since time immemorial, can never be recovered. And this letter is the one you have to have to cross the northern border. But the situation is not reciprocal, for never in his life will the gringo tourist recover the letter that is missing in English, or French, or German; none the less, he will cross the border as often as he wants for as long as he wants, to the point that it will lose its materiality.

9. See Gérard Noiriel, *La Tyrannie du national: Le droit d'asile en Europe (1793–1993)* (Paris: Calmann-Lévy, 1991).

10. On citizenship as a status in current international space, see Étienne Balibar, 'L'Europe des citoyens', in *Les Étrangers dans la cité: Expériences européenes*, ed. Olivier Le Cour Grandmaison and Catherine Wihtol de Wenden (Paris: La Découverte, 1993), pp. 192–208. [The equation of the terms is sufficiently strong that in contemporary American usage citizenship most often covers both concepts. Under the word *citizen*, the *American Heritage Dictionary* (Boston: Houghton Mifflin, 1992) lists 'citizen', 'national', and 'subject' as synonyms, commenting: 'the central meaning shared by these nouns is a person owing allegiance to a nation or state and entitled to its protection'. In Balibar's usage, *nationality* is the *status* of belonging, generally in an exclusive fashion, to a particular nation, by birth or naturalization; *citizenship* has a more active sense, designating rights and in particular a 'right to politics'. – Trans.]

11. Immanuel Kant, *De mundi sensibilis atque intelligiblis forma et principiis* (Inaugural Dissertation, 1770), sec. I:2, iii; translated as 'On the Form and Principles of the Sensible and the Intelligible World', in *Theoretical Philosophy, 1755–1770*, trans. and ed. David Walford (Cambridge: Cambridge University Press, 1992), p. 382: 'entirety, which is the absolute totality of its component parts'.

12. See Régis Debray, *Christophe Colomb, le visiteur de l'aube, suivi des Traités de Tordesillas* (Paris: La Différence, 1991).

13. See Ernst Kantorowicz, '*Pro Patria Mori* in Medieval Political Thought', in *Selected Studies* (Locust Valley, NY: J. J. Augustin, 1965), pp. 308–24.

14. [Pierre Méhaignerie, Garde des sceaux (Minister of Justice) in 1993, had proposed a sentence of 'perpétuité réelle', that is, life without parole, in cases of the murder of children aggravated by rape, torture, or other 'barbaric acts'. – Trans.]

15. The question is often posed as to exactly what constitutes the internal link, which is historically manifest but theoretically enigmatic, between French education and colonization, both of which are symbolized by the name of Jules Ferry. I believe that this link passes through the religious institution of the border. In the nineteenth century, the border of the French nation, indissolubly ideal and real, is a double border: a European contour (the 'hexagon', the 'natural borders' of the Rhine, the Alps, and the Pyrenees) and a global contour (the limits of the French Empire, an eminently 'republican' empire, a new Roman Empire). These two contours are infinitely close by right but infinitely distant in practice (not only because thousands of miles separate them, but because one encloses French citizens and the other essentially French subjects, referred to as 'natives'). The interstice between them, coloured pink on old French globes, is the zone of missions, where the recruitment of soldiers for the defence of the mother country has as its counterpart the diffusion of a sacred heritage of civilization: the Rights of Man, the French language, universal secularism. This allows us better to understand the forms that the battle against

'fundamentalism' [*l'intégrisme*] can take in certain of the Republic's schools, for example, episodes that might seem disproportionate, such as the unanimous mobilization of a junior high school's teachers against the admission to the Republican school of a few young girls more or less voluntarily wearing 'Islamic veils', or the obdurate resistance to granting excuses from gym class, which in other cases are to be had for the asking. This is because the internal border is at stake: the 'Empire' no longer exists, but its ideas is still present, as is the ghost of its 'subjects', with their 'superstitions' or 'fanaticisms'. Every veil that crosses the door of a school above which is inscribed 'Liberty, Equality, Fraternity' (to which we have long since learned to add the words 'free, secular, and mandatory') is the proof, not only that we had to renounce the empire, which is fundamentally secondary, but above all that we had to withdraw from it without having accomplished the mission that we believed we were fulfilling there: liberating peoples from their ignorance and their intolerance, teaching the French version of secular religion to all.

16. Rémi Brague, *Europe, la voie romaine* (Paris: Critérion, 1992).

17. [In thermodynamics, the triple point designates the relation between temperature and pressure at which solid, liquid, and vapour states coexist in equilibrium. – Trans.]

18. For some complementary developments, see Étienne Balibar, 'Quelles frontières de l'Europe?' in *Penser l'Europe à ses frontières*, Géophilosophie de l'Europe/Carrefour des Littératures européennes de Strasbourg (La Tour d'Aigues: Éditions de l'Aube, 1993), pp. 90–100.

19. Christian Jacob, 'Le contour et la limite: Pour une approche philosophique des cartes géographiques', in *Frontières et limites*, ed. Christian Descamps (Paris: Éditions Centre Pompidou, 1991).

20. Martin Bernal, *Black Athena: The Afroasiatic Roots of Classical Civilization* (New Brunswick, NJ: Rutgers University Press, 1987).

(*Translated by James Swenson*)

6

Is a European Citizenship Possible?

The following reflections do not in any way claim to exhaust the question of European citizenship; rather, they address key elements of the question in order to determine its implications. This approach, while admittedly hypothetical, is dictated not only by the prospective nature of the seminars for which I developed these ideas, but also by the conviction that today these themes – 'the Europe of citizens', 'European citizenship' and 'citizenship in Europe' – cannot be the object of purely normative juridical treatment (at the legislative or regulative level), nor of deductive treatment which proceeds from a pre-existing concept of citizenship and of the citizen. Above all, these themes require reflection on the stakes involved in their articulation, their tensions, and their contradictions.

This approach does not deny the importance of the juridical aspects of the problem of citizenship in general, but refuses to frame its inquiry in terms of a preconceived form or given procedure. We must avoid prescribing, or in some way pre-forming, the question in terms of the existing concept of 'constitution', since this concept is bound up with a given period and the very type of citizenship which is in question. If a European citizenship is truly to emerge in the future then the very notion of constitutional order will have to change profoundly.

The particular conjuncture in which we take up the question of European citizenship constitutes a *proclaimed* historical turning point. In fact, it was proclaimed at least twice: first by the definitive moment in the political construction of Europe. Since the official adoption of the plans to institute free circulation (that is, during the 1970s; see Giannoulis 1992; Costa-Lascoux 1992), the dawn of a new era in the history of the European nations has in some ways been predetermined. The millenarian idea which circulated held that this moment of truth would soon be at hand (in 1993 or 1994), and that we would soon see its effects – or, if it came to pass, would feel its tensions or crises. However, the turning point was again proclaimed when political changes occurred in Eastern Europe between 1988 and 1990, a change that several journalists and political scientists, particularly Ralph Dahrendorf (1992), called the 'Revolution of 1989'. The fall of Communism was interpreted as both producing a supplementary degree of historical necessity and calling for a more precise realization of European citizenship, including as a corollary a new balance of forces in the world and the emergence of a new, more 'continental' level of the crystallization of power.

The most striking fact about the past three years, however, is that things have not gone precisely according to plan. This is not to say that a new era is not dawning, but precisely that it will not follow the path that was envisioned. Consider the sudden awareness of contradictions – between European nations, between social groups within each nation, between European 'political classes' and the '*peuple*' or 'popular classes' – which resulted from the Treaty of Maastricht. The vicissitudes of the Treaty's ratification are precisely at the origin of the proliferation of debates on democracy and citizenship at the European level. Despite their very different forms from one country to the next, these debates explicitly addressed the question of sovereignty, only to find that there were distinctly differing views on the political and monetary unification of Europe. Considered by some to be confused and savage, by others to be a saving grace, the reaffirmation of this sovereignty constituted the implicit tenor of the demonstrations of the independence of public opinion against the decisions made by governments and experts. But what is more, with the fall of the 'Wall' the external boundaries of the new European entity were again being questioned. The very real possibility of this entity giving rise to constitutional crises and a questioning of national unity in certain member states (the United Kingdom, Italy, and so on) also cannot be dismissed today (Rusconi, 1993).

The conjuncture of the institution of 'European citizenship' and the status of extra-European Community immigration also presents itself in unforeseen terms: it is no longer simply a post-colonial question of interpenetration between 'North' and 'South', but also a general problematization of the notion of *border* in the world. Without warning, Europeans have emerged from a bipolar world of 'two blocs' whose antagonism overdetermined all the borders. But what are the geopolitical borders of today, and what exactly is a border?

Such a situation allows for several interpretative possibilities. One might think that the debate on European citizenship is the result of a process begun long ago which has finally found its political and reflective moment (see, for example, Rosanvallon 1992). One might also decide that this debate is symptomatic of the 'catastrophic' turn that history is taking in Europe today. Each perspective has its merits, so that the paradigms generate the expectation of a pro-claimed turning point, then react to unforeseen catastrophe. Per-haps the most interesting aspect of this is the discrepancy between the paradigms and the objects which confront them.

Thus, the situation demands a radical historicization of both the present and the past. Nothing could be more demanding, precisely because of the rapid transformation of the terms of the debate. The causes of this rapid transformation are not reducible to European construction, which, in many ways, is nothing more than an attempt to respond to the profoundly altered conditions of the existence of the state. Rather, they reveal a broader category of political ques-tions, notably those concerning collective identity, the role of popular participation and representation in the economy of power, and the weaving of the *communal* and the *social* into the fabric of concrete politics. Before debating the new relational mode between collective behaviours and the organization of public authorities required by supra-national construction, we must understand why the turning point in European history coincides with a crisis of the very notion of the citizen, precipitated to some degree by its entire history. The current debates are haunted by the search for a paradigm in which cultural pluralism will no longer be residual or subordinate, but constitutive. They are only partially aware of the need to re-examine each implication, each justification, of the equation (*citizenship* = *nationality*) = *sovereignty*. Even if this equation is no longer considered sacrosanct by everyone, it none the less operates at the basis of the organization of civic rights, and dominates even the prospect of an evolution. Very often, the idea of supra-national citizenship has no meaning other than the displacement to a 'higher' order of the very characteristics of national citizenship.

Models of Citizenship

There are, to be sure, several historical models of citizenship. According to the historical and sociological tradition of the nineteenth and twentieth centuries, these models were divided into two main categories: ancient citizenship and modern citizenship. The citizen of Antiquity, inscribed in a network of community *affiliations* which constituted the very structure of the city, was characterized by his *objective* personal status, be it hereditary or quasi-hereditary. Modern citizenship, founded on both *subjective* and *universalist* principles (universalism of individual rights: in particular, the right to political participation; universal suffrage; universalism of opportunity of access to the elite; generalized education; universalism of proclaimed democratic ideals, whatever the real degree of their institution), must nevertheless be inaugurated by a *positive* institution. This institution corresponds historically to the European nation-state, later exported throughout the world through colonization and decolonization.

The shift from the ancient model to the modern model of citizenship would thus constitute a reversal of primacy between the community pole and the individual pole. This reversal, however, would only further demonstrate the formal continuity, that is, the permanence of a *rule of closure* or *autarky*, associated with citizenship. By definition, citizenship can exist only where we understand a notion of city to exist – where fellow citizens and foreigners are clearly distinguished in terms of rights and obligations in a given space. This formal distinction is in no way threatened by the existence of intermediary categories such as *metoikoi* (foreigners living permanently in Athens and enjoying special rights) and residents, provided that those who belong to these subcategories do not enjoy those rights of sovereignty reserved for full citizens. In this respect, the modern *nation* is still – and must still consider itself – a *city*. The move from ancient to modern citizenship is thus marked by a continuity, that of the principle of exclusion, without which there would be no community and thus no politics, with the community constituting both the defining interest and the legitimating principle in either model.

Historical reality, however, is more complicated than these models. The global antithesis of the ancient city and the modern city is invoked either in terms of a return to Antiquity, a reconsecration of the civic community, or, on the contrary, as proof of the irreversible trends towards individualization of social relations. This antithesis conceals many unresolved problems.

We might begin by accounting for the tendential oppositions at the very heart of the ancient conception of citizenship. Nicolet (1976, 1982) astutely demonstrated what distinguishes the Roman Republican city, even more the Imperial city, from the Greek polis: Rome tended to unify, under a single authority, the ensemble of those who shared the same 'culture'. Yet Rome was led to conceptualize and practise this participation or affiliation as if it were infinitely capable of extension – not to all human individuals, but to some individuals from all walks of life who, having acquired and hereditarily maintained the status of citizen, would form the ruling class of the empire. Hence the possibility of tracing analogies with either the modern nation or empires to come, especially empires which have as their centre colonialist nation-states such as Holland, Britain, and France, which will also be states conferring rights [*Rechsstaat*].

The fact that the Roman state could have unified and motivated several hundred thousands of citizens over several centuries without exploding ... is a unique phenomenon in ancient history. Well before the France of the declining monarchy and the Revolution, or the England of 1688, Rome was able to transform Italy into a nation, the first of its kind in history – a nation which responded, two thousand years before its articulation, to the famous definitions elaborated by French nationalism: a 'consent to live together' [*vouloir vivre ensemble*]. It is altogther indicative of the Roman political system that the last war and the only war fought by Rome against the Italians, a civil war, was fought against a people who were knocking harder and harder on the door of the city and who, in doing so, finally got it open. (Nicolet 1976: 514)

We must also, however, consider the history of 'citizenship' and the 'bourgeoisie' [*Bürgertum*] of the medieval town and of the confederations, the principalities, and the monarchies of the *ancien régime*, which tends precisely to problematize a global comparison between the ancient city and the modern city. It is easy to understand why: such a citizenship always represents an equilibrium between autonomy and submission. In other words, as opposed to the theoretical implications of national citizenship at least, citizenship construed as such corresponds for the collectivity [*le peuple*] to a *limited* sovereignty (see, for example, Ullmann 1966; Dilcher 1980). And conversely, it is even easier to understand why, in the case of France and elsewhere, the identification of the 'rights of man' with the 'rights of the citizen', and the winning of popular sovereignty under the name of nation, have led to the strong association in the collective imaginary between *citizenship* (the universal right to politics) and *nationality*, even if the signification of the latter term has changed profoundly over time. This has not prevented different analysts (among them Barret-Kriegel 1988) from trying to inscribe the republican form in the continuity of this model, in a profoundly Tocquevillian manner.

These considerations are essential to this discussion for at least two reasons. On the one hand, it is only through a study of the traces left over time by the Roman Empire and the medieval monarchies that we can understand the formation of the modern ideal of cosmopolitanism (of which the internationalism of workers and socialist intellectuals is, in the last analysis, simply a variant). Constitutive or legal citizenship in modern bourgeois nations, which is national, is ideally referred to a cosmopolitan concept of the unity of humankind. Modern cosmopolitanism is to real politics what the rights of man are to the rights of citizens: a utopian future, nourished by the memory of a lost unity. Yet, for such a community of citizens, the idea and practice of a limited sovereignty within the framework of a 'world order' which imposes constraints on the community even as it confers representation and rights certainly does not belong purely and simply to the past. It seems, on the contrary, that whatever form – neo-imperialist or democratic and transnational – the reorganization of relations between states takes after the Cold War (during which limited sovereignty was practised but not admitted, within each bloc), this reorganization is surely the political and juridical horizon of globalization.

Which Rule of Exclusion for Europe?

Significantly, though, all prospects of supra-national or transnational citizenship immediately create a formidable difficulty. Clearly, it is not enough simply to define the new 'community of citizens' as an addition to the pre-existing national communities, one which would add nothing to the already established concepts of citizenship, or would signify that the various national citizenships were henceforth combined, absorbed one into the other or into one citizenship that had become dominant. Must we, then, proceed in reverse to the normative definition of a 'co-citizenship' [*concitoyenneté*] that history did not produce as such, even if it conferred on the concept a certain number of justifications? This is what seems to happen. We look for this definition in a purely artificial perspective (the conclusion of a new 'contract' between Europeans), or rather, by supporting it with naturalist elements – that is, the community of culture and of common history rather than lineage in the strict sense.

Nevertheless, the stumbling block is always the same: it is the need to *formulate a rule of exclusion* founded on rights and principles. Desite the definition proposed in 1991 by the European Commission and employed in the drafting of the Treaty of Maastricht ('S/He is a citizen of the union who possesses the nationality of a member state' [Heymann-Doat 1991], we cannot be satisfied with simply reinstating the exclusions that already exist (something to this effect: 'European citizens' will be those who *were not excluded* from their respective national citizenships). What is implicitly required, in reference to a whole series of contemporary experiences (some truly traumatic) and of moral principles, and under the pressure of exacerbated interests, real or imaginary, is a *supplementary* rule of exclusion which properly belongs to the new citizenship of the post-national era.

This difficulty manifests itself acutely in terms of the citizenship of immigrants. Included in this category, and beyond the different denominations in use today, are all the extra-Community workers and their families who have taken up residence for one or more generations in European countries, as well as at least some of the refugees seeking asylum. It is difficult to decide if this is a cause or an effect of the current resurgence of xenophobic sentiments in the European Community. Despite the naturalization procedures (facilitated very unequally from country to country) and the restrictions on immigration officially imposed by most of the countries in the mid-1970s, it is estimated that immigrants make up 8 per cent of the population of Europe (Schnapper 1992). Pre-existing distinct national citizenships can, at least without apparent inconsistency, keep in an extraneous status, on their own territory, foreign individuals who entered that territory at a given moment provided, first, that these individuals are neither too numerous nor too stable, and second, that they do not integrate themselves either into a large number of institutions – academic, medical, or those related to local government – or into economic as well as sporting and cultural enterprises. But the aporia is obvious as soon as entire groups of 'foreigners' appear tendentially, due to anticipation or adaptation, to be typical of a *new sociability and citizenship*, which is concurrent with national sociability and citizenship. From that point on, 'immigrants' of extra-Community origin risk appearing as quintessential *Europeans*. This is not without analogy to the way Germany and France, during the last century, assimilated Jews, who, although not ascribed regional affiliation (rootedness), passed for quintessential *national* citizens.

If a new citizenship created on European soil does not succeed in conceiving itself and putting itself into practice collectively as though it were open by design, then it is going to have to decide, and theoretically posit, that citizenship *does not extend to some* of the individuals who none the less occupy this soil, and that in this sense, it 'separates them from the others' according to a certain *generic* criterion similarly applicable in all countries. This poses grave problems of definition if we do not want to consider explicitly the criteria of lineage or geographic origin. This would lead to *forging* the purely fabricated category of 'non-citizen residents in Europe', implicating citizenship in the constitution of *apartheid*, at the very moment when it proclaims progress in universalism.

What, then, is the alternative? It can only be the coupling of a definition of civic community with a principle of openness, even possibly a regulated openness. Such a coupling would acknowledge not only that the European entity and identity are the result of a convergence of groups originating from all parts of the world on European soil, but also, specifically, that citizenship defines itself in principle as a non-exclusive membership.

This idea is logically enigmatic and unprecedented, even if it seems to resemble certain personal statuses of multinationality or the principles of naturalization in nations with traditions of immigration like France, and especially Australia or nations in North and South America. Nations of emigration have, on the contrary, rejected this idea, traumatized as they were by the loss of their 'substance'. There is a great deal to say about this. Modern statuses of multinationalism are always strictly individual, and do not confer much power. In this sense they confirm rather, by virtue of individual exceptions, the ideology of the *affiliation* of individuals to their nation-state, and the practice of their administrative *appropriation*. For their part, nations of immigration have most often used their ethnic quotas to regulate procedures for accepting new citizens, and symbolically overdetermined their citizens' surrender of their nationality or culture of origin. In this way, they redraw their borders precisely where they risk becoming relativized. The paradoxes are quite profound, because in one sense modern communities of citizens owe their historic permanence solely to diverse processes of assimilation, that is to say, to the sum of the practices used to get around the principle of exclusion, to which these communities theoretically object. Here in France it would entail a re-evaluation of this principle itself, the ultimate purpose being institutionally to inscribe a historical and sociological *fait accompli.*

Rights and Statuses

There is more. The alternative mentioned above, at least as the outline of the problem – the constitution of a type of *apartheid* or the transition to a largely *open,* transnational citizenship – is accompanied by another problem which concerns the contractual founding of democratic citizenship and its relationship to the notion of status. *Status or contract*: this old dilemma takes on new meaning today. One could argue that the question will inevitably resurface in the two hypotheses envisioned. Simply stated, in the European apartheid hypothesis, 'status' will be a pseudo-hereditary privilege which operates according to the law of all or nothing. This would permit restricting the extension of citizenship, and of all juridical and political recognition of the sociological reality of immigration. In the hypothesis of open European citizenship, however, status will be the expression of a regulation, of a political and administrative control exercised over the stages and modalities of the openness and thereby susceptible to variations in degree.

For all that has been said, I do not think that we can simply follow the jurists and political scientists (e.g. Leca 1992) who define *citizenship primarily as a status,* which is tantamount to nationality. What allows for relative continuity between the various modes of institution of citizenship, and permits us to understnd the theoretical and always problematic links that they maintain with concepts such as democracy and popular sovereignty, is never merely the reference to a *communauté*. It is, rather, the reference to a *commune* (in English, commonwealth rather than community; in German, *Gemeinde* rather than *Gemeinschaft*). It is the fact that the notion of citizen – derived from an initial reference to insurrection, as in the case of France, or to the right to resist, as in the case of the United States; in short, to 'constituent power' (Negri 1992) – is the expression of a collective political capacity to 'constitute the state' or the public space. Hence, it is this notion that provides the link between the idea of citizenship and those of equality, of liberty (for which I have coined the word *égaliberté*), which constitutes the main theme of its historical dialectic. I do not mean to reduce this dialectic to a progression in the sense of universalization, but it seems to me incontestable that the telos, or the ideal of the 'free community of equals', constitutes one of the permanent poles of the dialectic.

We should agree, however, that if citizenship never defines itself according to a simple matter of status – thus in an inegalitarian or hierarchical manner – this position is nevertheless immediately reintroduced; not only externally through the distinction between citizens and foreigners, but also internally. Citizenship coresponds to the constitution of a differentiated society, and to the functioning of a state. Thus, at the very least, citizenship implies a distinction between those who govern and those who are governed, and a separation of public service and civil society. The importance assumed by the immigrant worker in modern capitalist societies leads in effect to this: that inequality of status is projected simul-taneously into the national political space from two sides – through nationality and the social division of labour – and that the demand or request for equality is recast in terms of a set of movements and social rights which have been more or less acquired, more or less incorporated into the concept of citizenship, independently of ethnic-national origin.

This historical tension between the equality pole and the status (or hierarchical) pole effectively generates the multiple resonances of the concept of citizenship, which is impossible to confine *a priori* to a single form, or to declare conclusively perfected. The history of the struggles and compromises that this multiplicity masks, however, has never been adequately documented. This is due primarily to the myth of continuous progress towards civic participation, typical of the philosophy of the Enlightenment and of its heir in this respect, the Romantic philosophy of history. It is also due to the correlative illusion, sustained by the political science and sociology of twentieth-century institutions, of an irreversible decadence which would lead to apathy, individualism, and collective clientelism.

Here I would like to put forth the hypothesis that two movements are occurring simultaneously. The first leads from a conceptualization of *citizenship as a status* to the conceptualization of *social citizenship* as a producer of status. From an initial situation in which institutions specify the more or less restrictive conditions of a full exercise of civic rights, or of participation in the political sphere (a situation which persists in the modern city in the case of 'passive citizens', and especially the citizenship of women), we move to a situation in which, the universality of civil rights being presupposed, the capacity of citizen brings about the recognition of specific rights, and notably of social rights. The primary interest of the now classic definition of citizenship advanced by T.H. Marshall (1965) is to present citizenship as a historical movement whose *modus operandi* resides not so much in the realization of a selfsame formal concept of the citizen in historically successive spaces or frames as in the incorporation into this concept of new functions and spheres of involvement, which then transform it. This is the ideal type of transition from civil citizenship to political citizenship, and then to social citizenship. However, the greatest difficulty with this schema, which the current conditions of European political construction and, more generally, the state of politics in the world reveal very clearly, is its profoundly teleological nature. It immediately presupposes a linear and irreversible progress – beyond the delays or the unevenness of development – as well as a compatibility of principles between the different aspects of citizenship successively put into place. Consequently, not only is it out of the question here that social citizenship should go hand in hand with the limitation and decline of civil rights and political rights, but there can be no question of contradictions, even potential contradictions, between the conditions that permit the realization of different aspects of citizenship at any given moment.

The second movement is one theorized notably by Hegel as constitution of the state and by Weber as rationalization. It leads from a *right to politics* – exercised in an undifferentiated manner, but by a socially or territorially limited collectivity – to a *participation* in the activities of the state and civil society which becomes larger and larger, but also more and more differentiated. Such a participation then takes the form of an equilibrium between multiple administrative posts and multiple non-exclusive groups (in contemporary parliamentary regimes those of the electorate, politicos [*hommes politiques*], experts, militants, national or multinational lobbyists).

At least in theory, the moment of insurrection during the French Revolution, symbolized by the work of the Convention, constitutes a reconciliation between the two opposing exigencies of, on the one hand, lack of differentiation of political functions (which grants absolute power to the sovereignty of the people), and, on the other, virtually limitless extension of the civic collectivity. It is certainly not by chance that the Marxist tradition, while critiquing the juridical-political ideology dominting this popular form of representation, never stopped trying to find it in practice and in the movement of the historical emancipation of the masses themselves. Nor is it by chance that the most radical contemporary theoreticians of the decline of classical sovereignty – for example, Foucault in France – have continued to take the opposite point of view.

From this perspective, does the question of European citizenship take an unprecedented form? Perhaps. In the light of the discussions for and against supra-nationality, we should not pass too quickly over necessary comparisons with the preceding processes of which it inevitably bears the traces. Consider, for example, the construction of the US federal government and its various reprercussions in the world; or, more importantly, the construction and deconstruction of the 'citizenship of empire' on a global scale in the British Commonwealth and the French Empire, with their more or less lasting successors. Another process comes to mind: the construction and decline of Soviet citizenship, since in theory it combined universal openness with the recognition of individual and collective social rights, and made these principles the basis of the existence of civil rights and political participation, thus inverting, in a certain sense, Marshall's ideal-typical order. Nevertheless, the fact remains that today we are faced with an extreme form of the tension between the equality and the status aspects of citizenship, a situation from which it seems difficult to emerge without a profound redefinition of both aspects.

The State and Counter-powers

Why are we in this criticial situation? I could give strategic reasons which bear witness to the transformations brought about by economic globalization. The new phase of centralization of the movements of capital, hierarchization of manual labour, and distribution of territorial resources makes the most of the revolution in communication, and engages in a competitive relationship with the nation-states. The fall of historical Communism has profoundly modified this situation. After this event, the Western European Union found itself in a quasi-imperial situation, since it was the only supra-national construction in Europe. As a result, however, the question of the margins or markets of this quasi-empire, in terms of business and of potential integration, becomes crucial. With this question come others concerning the stages, modalities, and degrees of integration of Eastern Europeans into European citizenship, or at least into the field of equality relative to civic rights in Europe. Is the Yugoslavian civil war not, in many respects, a 'social war' in the Roman sense of the term – one in which 'allies' fight among themselves? In this new situation, a triple constraint exists: colonial heritage, the importation of cheap labour, reunification of the 'two halves' of Europe. Under terms such as associates, refugees or migrants, it tends to define 'others' who are not completely 'foreign' as being neither outside nor inside in relation to the economy and to the ideal type of affiliation to the community, and sometimes even to is institutions.

From this perspective, European citizenship always risks returning to a definition in terms of status rather than contract. This will be due not so much to an essential equation with nationality as to the way in which, as a criterion for access to civil and political rights, and to the social rights which have historically become their counterpart in the national-social state, European citizenship will find itself at the intersection of multiple processes of differentiation. Locally, national citizenship is complemented at the bottom by diverse 'partial' or 'approximate' citizenships, whereas on a global scale – along with US and, perhaps tomorrow, Japanese citizenship – the passport of the European Community citizen tends to function as a guarantee of privileged personal status in the open space which corresponds to the global economy. This is the modern equivalent of the *Civis romanus sum* which Saint Paul invoked before the praetor of Judaea.

By a symmetry inscribed throughout the history of the concept of citizen, however, the emphasis on the status and hierarchical aspect of citizenship allows us to reformulate the question in terms of its egalitaian aspect. This question never comes up in the abstract, but always in terms of the characteristics of an existing state, in a dialectic of representation and conflict. Experience teaches us in this context that democratic citizenship is not so much the type of citizenship which elides the state in the name of a hypothetically autonomous civil society (that is to say, which would exist completely outside the nexus of state institutions), as the type which manifests itself in the constitution of strong *counter-powers* which, in the face of the autonomization of state apparatuses (removed as they are from the average citizen), exercise on these apparatuses a certain constraint, repression, or supervision. Inasmuch as the construction of counter-powers is not purely defensive or reactive, it tends also towards a collective control exercised by individuals over the social powers on which they depend for their very existence. Is not one of the main reasons for the 'preference' in democracies for the organization of public authorities the fact that these authorities (at least in principle, and in contrast to private powers) are less likely to escape the control of those whom they control? It is fairly clear, however, that in the recent operation of most administrations and governments, privatization prospers under the guise of the public.

How, then, can we broach the question of controlling the controllers, or of publicizing [*une publicisation de*] the exercise of powers at a European level? In this context, once again, the paradox is obvious. As we have seen, the 'European state' is a phantom. Officially denied sovereignty, it continues nevertheless to develop its domains of intervention and its skill at negotiating with the centres of economic decision-making: the set of state practices whose precise centre of legitimacy, authority, and public nature is a mystery to the very individuals who theoretically occupy it. In so far as the current insidious crisis of European institutions has exacerbated this situation, it manifests itself rather as a regression inasmuch as it reactivates the competition between the apparatuses of the nation-states and the embryo of a supra-national apparatus, in which each pole attempts to present itself as the pre-eminent site of sovereignty.

One of the reasons for this, obviously, is that nationalist discourse considers equally unacceptable both the idea of limited sovereignty for states (even when it corresponds closely to practice) and that of a politics of the masses, using different means of representation and pressure to limit the autonomy of state apparatuses and of the ruling classes or castes. Note that such a discourse is liable to include hegemonic interests as well as defensive reactions to the erosion of the national-social state. Unfavourable economic conditions do not adequately explain the incapacity of trade unions, and more generally of the workers' and socialist movements, make the kind of breakthrough that would enable them to organize their political thought and action on the same scale as those of the ruling classes.

The collective control of powers in the European context is currently all the more unreal in that the constitutional postulate of collective identity masks an administrative proliferation which does not present itself as a state. In fact, the displacement of decisions to the European level is accompanied by an extreme disequilibrium of possibilities for different social categories to use the political and administrative apparatus in the service of their respective interests. The notion that the state is, in general, neutral – whether this is true or not – is thus quickly losing momentum. This must obviously be read in conjunction with the fact that the construction of European citizenship is taking place at the same time as an extraordinarily brutal rupture of continuity in the history of social movements – and especially the workers' movement, whose relationship with the state, characterized by both irreconcilable and reconcilable conflict for more than a century, constituted one of the basic principles behind the emergence of counter-powers.

This situation, which may appear to be a vicious circle, is not without import since again, in Western as in Eastern Europe, the signification of the terms *peuple*, *Volk*, or *narod* as community, affiliation, or identity (which I have called *fictive ethnicity*) prevails over their signification as general will and egalitarian collective power. The problem has no obvious solution, but this must not prevent us from asking if the countervailing aspect of a limited sovereignty – including the limitation of exclusive appropriation by states of their own nationals – would not reside precisely in a more public image for a more recognized exercise of counter-powers at different levels where decisions are henceforth focused. In this way one would constitute transnational political subjects according to national as well as transnational procedures, and not merely constitute citizens as national subjects.

Civic Duty, Patriotism and Nationalism

There is one final dimension of the problem to investigate: the role of the nation, constructed by the history of institutions, social struggles, and collective ordeals (transformed by the imaginary into founding events), in the civic and political formation of individuals. We could base our discussion here on a remarkable text by Rusconi (1993) on the Italian situation, in which the questions almost always have general import and find their analogues in the French context, or are relevant to the problems we have in common in the new European context. Such an analysis has no real French equivalent, although France could certainly do with one. Thus, we risk finding ourselves ill equipped to face the critical economic situations and political movements that have begun to bombard us. Do we see in nationalism the past or the future? This re-examination of a notion whose meaning seemed fixed has become the very condition of an understanding of politics. The risk of speculation is lower in this respect than the risk of remaining the prisoner of a lazy confrontation between the converse dogmatisms of national defence and supra-nationality.

The history of nation formation, and its interaction with the construction of the state and the phases of economic development, must lead to a veritable historicization of the nation-form, the correlative of the discussion of citizenship above. This in turn leads us to question – without an already formulated response – which alternative formations have been suppressed by the dominant formation in the past, and why such alternatives are re-emerging, with more or less violence, under the conditions of present-day globalization. In this respect, Italy is an extreme example, but it also attests to the fact that political crisis is not limited to the phenomena of the corruption and privatization of the state, or the transformation of the modes of communication and collectice representation. It is a crisis intrinsic to the *national-social state* (the real name of what we have labelled the welfare state), and to the concrete form of the institution of citizenship over the last fifty years. Whatever the very unequal – and sometimes seemingly false – degrees of its realization, the national-social state is an irreversible stage of nationality in the world. Under its old form, the national-social state has also become literally impossible in developed countries (to say nothing of elsewhere), geneating a crisis in the nation-form whose outcome remains indeterminate. Obviously, European construction, even if it becomes social, represents only one factor among others, one which generates its own alternatives.

Here, we have reached the point at which the problems raised by the state's loss of legitimacy and credibility, which can give rise throughout Europe to the phenomena of violence, nihilism and authoritatianism, merge with the fundamental questions of political philosophy and the philosophy of history. What relationship does a political democracy have with the existence of a *community conscious-ness* of its own citizens?

In this respect, Rusconi (1993) is fairly close to a kind of left Gaullism. From a philosophical point of view, he situates himself well within the Hegelian tradition, focusing on the need for democ-racy to actualize a new synthesis of civic universalism and historical rootedness, in order to reconstitute its sense of solidarity and responsibility. His polemical argument is rightly directed against ahistorical conceptions of citizenship, yet it seems to me insuffi-ciently historicized.

If democracy, as a system of living traditions, finds its expression in both the representation of the governed and the control of those who govern – by a sufficient appropriateness of the representation of the population's interests and ideas, and by a sufficient degree of popular control over the controllers themselves – it is never more than a fragile equilibrium between the functions of consensus and the functions of conflict. Ultimately, democracy lives on the inverse excesses of these functions. In this way, democracy depends at least as much upon *fortuna* as upon *virtù*, as much upon favourable circumstances as upon the initiative of the ruling class, the parties, and the citizens. If we want to understand history, it is essential that we do not exaggerate the importance of consensus to the detriment of conflict.

In saying this, I do not mean to resuscitate a reductive concep-tion of politics as the expression of class struggle. I want, rather, to ask that politics should be conceived in terms of its real conditions, ideological as well as social. In France, as in Italy, during about a thirty-year period, a certain degree of democracy was achieved, notably because the forces capable of mobilizing the mass of workers who considered themselves or were considered 'outside the system' [*extérieures*], or wanted to 'go beyond it', performed in it the *tribunitian function* of maintaining [*entretien*] social conflict (Lavau 1981). It is true that this 'exteriority' [*extériorité*] had a double meaning, laden with an awesome equivocality: social exteriority with respect to free-market capitalism; strategic exteriority in terms of an 'Western bloc', the repercussions of which were felt throughout the history of the working-class movements, even in cases where it did not admit to any allegiance with Communism.

To the vitality of democracy we must therefore apply Machiavelli's theorem rather than Hegel's theory, or we must at least correct one with the other. Again, the object is to understand the stakes and possible consequences of the crisis of the national-social state. We may well be astonished by the fact that the decline of the workers' movement and of class ideologies, which has both moral and economic sources, soon leads not to a triumph but to a crisis of their historical 'opposite' – unitary national feeling and the idea of civic community, as attested by the phenomena of disinterest in politics as well as outbursts of identity nationalism, or ethnicization of national consciouness. But these two phenomena probably constitute a single phenomenon. And since this is so, the most important task at hand is to rediscover for democracy more collective ideals, and a deeper entrenchment within libertarian and egalitarian movements that protest against the status quo.

These conditions have contributed to the current resurgence of discussions on patriotism. Rusconi approaches the question through a critical analysis of 'constitutional patriotism' [Verfassungspatriotismus], defended by Habermas in the debates on the revision of the German historical past [Historikerstreit], and again in the recent confrontations concerning the reform of the Federal Constitution and the right of asylum. Idealist though Habermas's perspective may appear, the question that he raised by publicly attacking stereotypes of political and historical normality which regard it as 'normal' for a nation to have its own unitary state is destined to remain topical for a long time (1992b). Patriotism is an affair of ideals. And it is precisely ideals capable of linking generations that are required for democratic politics today, however materialist it may want to consider itself. But there are no ideals without their share of repression, without latent contradictions which become sublimated.

Significantly, though, contrary to what we might hope, there are also ideals in nationalism, even in imperialist nationalism. The idea of the 'French nation', like that of the 'German nation', fed on an orgy of spiritualism in 1914. This fact is overlooked by all histories of European nationalism which consider their historical association with republican institutions an essential truth, or believe that they are able to distinguish between good (democratic, political) and bad (ethnic, exclusive, cultural) nationalisms. It is precisely when we deny any political equivalence between democratic nationalism and a nationalism of aggression and ethnic cleansing that it becomes indispensable to conduct a thorough analysis of their common ideological bases.

Just as we must agree to question the ambiguity of the references to the 'pact of the Resistance', we must agree to examine what affinities there might be between the 'heroic' activism of fascist *engagement* (at least at a certain point in time) and the 'moral' activism of *engagement* in the French or Italian Resistance. Such symmetries lead not to the conceptual amalgamation of these ideologies but, rather, to a better understanding of why political stereotypes have never sufficed in determining behaviour, and why at certain times choices, even risky ones, were necessary. The choices are no simpler today than they were in the past, because the signifiers and the imaginary of nationalism float between multiple usages and multiple levels: 'old' nation-states searching for a new role on the world stage; infra-national entities with their fictive ethnicity attached to their name – Flanders, Corsica, or Scotland; and supra-national entities. Indeed, a *European nationalism* does exist, and is more or less influential according to the historical conjuncture; it is a component of each of our political spaces, and has definitively displaced the old 'federalism'.

All of this affects the definition of citizenship and the ways in which citizenship is affected by immigration as well as by the conflict, or even the manipulations, caused by immigration. Recent debates, notably in France, have begun to generate reflection both on the effects of European construction and on the new character of immigration in Western Europe. What is important here – and this bears repeating – is not so much to propose a recasting of the equation *citizenship equals nationality*, or to transpose it on to the supra-national level, or, conversely, to proclaim it obsolete; but, rather, to go below the surface, to expose it as a problem rather than accept it as a given or a norm.

This equation, involving the nationalization of citizenship by the state and the evolution of the nation into a 'nation of citizens', could not have become essential and reconstituted itself periodically without a strong element of internal democracy, a productive tension between the idea of *peuple* as a community [*Ein Volk*] and the idea of *peuple* as a principle of equality and social justice [*das Volk*]. In short, this equation could not have lasted through the trauma of 'European civil wars' and the ordeal of class struggles without an element of *intensive* universalism (which requires non-discrimination between individuals), not simply extensive universalism (which seeks the uniformity of individuals). The crucial factor here is how this dynamic of universalism works in politics today. For the past ten years in France, the 'left of the left' have been suggesting that the stable, socially necessary presence of immigrants and their children will inevitably pose the problem of non-discrimination, and thus of their citizenship. It appears, however, that if this prediction was right, this development concealed a certain number of illusions; in particular, the illusion which consists in imagining that the idea of an expanded and non-exclusive citizenship would advance more easily at the two extreme positions of the institutional chain, just below and beyond the nation-state. These two positions are, to put it plainly, local collectivities (citizenship of residence) and European citizenship. In the present situation, regional nationalisms have, tendentially, become not less, but *more exclusive* than the nationalisms of the state, and here the example of the Italian Leagues sounds a warning. Furthermore, the organization of European citizenship begins through the presence of law enforcement and restrictions on obtaining the right to asylum (Schengen, Dublin), rather than through an expanded democratic participation. Consequently, it is precisely to the centre of the equation *citizenship equals nationality* (in the analysis and critique of the concept of 'community' that it defines) that reflection and research on the dynamics of transformation must lead.

The debate on European citizenship may well seem academic today, at least as seen from France, as if it had never been more than a utopia destined to give way sooner or later to the 'real' questions of politics. Yet in 1994, the Treaty of Maastricht came into effect. This marked an irreversible stage in the emergence of a new political entity. Beyond juridical formulas – sometimes deliberately equivocal – the definition of this new political entity still conceals no unanimity, either among national components, or within each one of them. But, *de facto*, it cannot leave unaltered the civil relations between the residents of the European space – nor, as a consequence, their personal and collective status. In this respect, it is only ostensibly paradoxical to maintain that the convergence of constitutional revisions (in Germany and Holland) and measures to control the influx of individuals across the 'community border' could, in the long run, have greater consequences than the persistent divergence of commercial and monetary politics, and the acceptance of a construction of Europe 'at multiple speeds'. For until all traces of the *Rechsstaat* have formally disappeared from our political space – and fortunately, this is still some way off – the *anti-citizenship* represented by regulating exclusion, or enhancing the power of apparatuses of repression without increasing the possibility of democratic control, implies a latent redefinition of citizenship itself. And the framework and presupposition of this redefinition, whether we like it or not, is the European space, which, little by little, is taking on the characteristics of a territory.

It is therefore even more urgent to keep open the dialectic of the different ideas suggested here, which, although necessarily related, are by no means synonymous: community and exclusion – a *citizenship of Europeans*, that is, identity of 'origin', and the prior national membership with which the French, Germans, Greeks and others enter into the sphere of community rights and obligations; a *European citizenship* – *citizenship in Europe*, that is, a 'Europe of citizens', meaning, above all else, a space of civic rights and their progression, which Europe would intend to advance; and finally, an open transnational citizenship to which European construction would – at least partly – be the key.

Note

This essay was originally presented in French at the Ministry of Research and Technology on 12 February 1993, at the Franco–European Research and Futurology Seminar on the State: Sovereignty, Finance and Social Issues. It has been published in French as 'Une citoyenneté européene est-elle possible?', in Étienne Balibar, *L'État, la finance et la social. Souveraineté nationale et construction européene*, ed. Brunot Théret (Paris: La Découverte, 1995), and in an amended and expanded version in Étienne Balibar, *Droit de cité. Culture et politique en démoncratie* (Paris: Éditions de l'aube, 1998).

References

Balibar, Étienne (1992a) *Les Frontières de la démocratie*. Paris: La Découverte.

—— (1992b) 'Internationalisme ou barbarie', *Lignes*, 17 (October): 21–42.

Balibar, Étienne and Immanuel Wallerstein (1991) *Race, Nation, Class: Ambiguous Identities*. London: Verso.

Balke, Friedrich, Rebekka Habermas, Patrizia Nanz and Peter Sillem, eds (1993) *Schwierige Fremdheit, über Integration und Ausgrenzung in Einwanderungaländerungsländern*. Frankfurt am Main: Fischer Taschenbuch Verlag.

Barrel-Kriegel, Blandine (1988) *L'état et les esclaves*, 2nd ed. Paris: Calmann-Lévy.

Costa-Lascoux, Jacqueline (1992) 'Vers une Europe des Citoyens', in J. Costa-Lascoux and P. Weil, eds, *Logiques d'États et immigrations*. Paris: Kimé.

Dahrendorf, Ralph (1990) *Reflections on the Revolution in Europe*. London: Chatto & Windus.

Dilcher, Gerhard (1908) 'Zum Bürgerbegriff im späteren Mittelhalter. Versuch einer Typologie am Beispiel von Frankfurt am Main', in J. Fleckenstein and K. Stackmann, eds, *Über Bürger, Stadt und Staädtische Literatur im Spätmittelalter*. Göttingen: Abhandlungen der Akademie der Wissenchaften.

Foucault, Michel (1988) *Politics, Philosophy, Culture: Interviews and Other Writings, 1977–1984*, Trans. Alan Sheridan. New York: Routledge.

Giannoulis, Christina (1992) *Die Idee des 'Europa der Bürger und ihre Bedeutung für den Grundrechtsschutz*. Ph.D. dissertation, Universität des Saarlandes; Europa-Institut, Sektion Rechtswissenschaft.

Habermas, Jürgen (1992a) 'Cittadinaze e identità nazionale', in *Morale, Diritto, Politica*. Turin: Einaudi.

—— (1992b) 'Die zweite Lebenslüge der Bundesrepublik: Wir sind wieder "normal" geworden', *Die Zeit*, 11 December.

Heymann-Doat, Arlette (1993) 'Les institutions européenes et la citoyenneté', In O. Le Cour Grandmaison and C. Wihtol de Wenden, eds, *Les Étrangers dans la cité. Expériences européennes.* Paris: La Découverte/Ligue des Droits de l'Homme.

'*Historikerstreit.*' *Die Dokumentation der Kontroverse am die Einzigartigkeit der nazional-sozialistischen Judenvernichtung* (1987). Munich: Piper Verlag.

Julien-Laferriére, François (1993) 'Préface', in *Frontières due droit, frontières des droits. L'introuvable statut de la 'zone internationale'.* Paris: L'Harmattan/ANAFE.

Lavau, Georges (1981) *À quoi sert le parti communiste français?* Paris: Librairie Arthème Fayard.

Leca, Jean (1992) 'Nationalité et citoyenneté dans l'Europe des Immigrations', in J. Costa-Lascoux and P. Weil, eds, *Logiques d'États et immigrations.* Paris: Kimé.

Marshall, T.H. (1965) 'Citizenship and Social Class', in T.H. Marshall with an introduction by Seymour Martin Lipset, *Class, Citizenship, and Social Development.* New York: Anchor.

Negri, Antonio (1999) *Insurgencies: Constituent Power and the Modern State,* trans. Maurizia Boscagh. Minneapolis and London: University of Minnesota Press.

Nicolet, Claude (1976: 2nd rev. ed) *Le Métier de citoyen dans la Rome républicaine.* Paris: Gallimard.

—— (1982) 'Citoyenneté française et citoyenneté romaine: essai de mise en perspective', in *La nozione di 'romano' tra cittadinanza e universalità. Da Roma alla Terza Roma.* Roma: Documenti e Studi, Edizioni Scientifiche Italiane.

Noiriel, Gérard (1992) *Population, immigration et identité nationale en France, XIXe–XXe siècle.* Paris: Hachette.

Reberioux, Madeleine (1993) 'Préface', in O. Le Cour Grandmaison and C. Wihtol de Wenden, eds, *Les Étrangers dans la cité. Expériences européennes.* Paris: La Découverte/Ligue des Droits de l'Homme.

Rosanvallon, Pierre (1992) 'Préface', in Jean-Marc Ferry and Paul Thibaud, eds, *Discussion sur l'Europe.* Paris: Calmann-Lévy/Fondation Saint-Simon.

Rusconi, Gian Enrico (1993) *Se cessiamo di essere una nazione, Tra etnodemocrazie regionali e cittadinanza europea.* Bologna: Il Mulino.

Schnapper, Dominique (1992) *L'Europe des immigrés.* Paris: François Bourin.

Ullmann, Walter (1966) *The Individual and Society in the Middle Ages.* Baltimore, MD: Johns Hopkins University Press.

Van Gunsteren, Herman (1993) 'Contemporary Citizenship and Plurality'. Paper presented at the workshop on 'Citizenship and Plurality' at the Joint Sessions of the European Consortium for Political Research, Leiden University, 2–7 April.

(*Translated by Christine Jones*)

7

Violence, Ideality and Cruelty[1]

To put the terms *violence* and *ideality* together is to draw our attention to a series of paradoxical questions. I want to examine two reciprocal propositions: (1) that violence is, of necessity, part of what we might call 'the economy of ideality' (just as there is an economy of salvation, that is, part of its conditions and effects); (2) that ideality is part of the economy of violence, although we must admit that it is never its only determining factor.

If these propositions are true, there must be a profound ambivalence in the relationship between violence and ideality (a generic term in which, for the time being, I include ideas, ideals, idealizations), and a profound ambivalence in each of them. As a result, we cannot conduct a *simple* discussion of the problem of violence, nor find a universal 'solution' to it. Something will remain irreducibly problematic or ambiguous, if not immutable. We all assume, more or less, that we have a desire or tendency to escape violence, to reduce its forms and lower its level – to 'civilize customs' [*mores*], as Norbert Elias would put it; and this cannot be achieved without implementing ideals, idealizing and sublimating some of our own propensities. If my propositions are true, any stance that is taken, any move that is made, *against violence* (and this is certainly an essential part of the 'political') will have to come to terms with its backlash.

Politics – civilization itself – cannot be reduced to a programme for the elimination of violence, even though the problem will always be with us.

No doubt we would all like to put an end to violence, but I would like to begin by considering how ambivalent our attitude is in this respect. This time 'our' refers to us, *intellectuals*. I shall take two brief examples.

Soon after the end of World War II, in an essay called 'Utopia and Violence' (1947), which became Chapter 18 of *Conjectures and Refutations*, Sir Karl Popper expressed his fears that the victory over Nazism would be followed not by a reduction of the level of violence in the world and in world politics but, on the contrary, by fresh outbreaks of barbarity. He referred to the fact that the anti-Nazi alliance, mainly the United States, had been led to borrow some of their enemies' weapons and methods, themselves using massive retaliation and extermination of civilian populations. He was explicitly thinking of the Hiroshima bombing, but what worried him even more was the prospect of a new wave of political and social utopias, of the 'Platonist' type, which would aim at transforming the world, and human nature itself, by deconstructing and reconstructing the whole fabric of society according to ideal principles of justice. He warned that, as ever, this would not be done without resorting to, or being led to using, some extremely violent means. Popper was by no means in favour of a simple conservatism, since he recognized that there was much on this earth that needed to be changed; he pleaded for a reformist policy, and advocated what he called realistic 'piecemeal social engineering'.

This is indeed a classical version of the critique of the *effets pervers* of idealism, one of which, paradoxically enough, can be found in a work which was not one of Popper's favourites: Hegel's description of the French Revolution and the Terror in his *Phenomenology of Spirit*. I am mentioning it, however, for another reason: if you read this text again, you may be struck by the fact that it is rhetorically organized around the repetition of such phrases as 'I hate violence'; 'Those who, like me hate violence, will agree that . . .', and so on. This produces an extraordinary short circuit of the discourse and metadiscourse, and thus of the author's exegesis and subjective position. In a sense Popper recognizes this himself, since he explains, for instance, that his anti-violence stance cannot ultimately be justified by rational arguments, only by a certain humanitarian bias.

My attention was especially drawn to the difficulty which is involved here, since I had just read an excellent paper by my colleague Phil Cohen from the University of East London, which dealt with the discourse of violent groups of so-called hooligans, whose favourite slogan is simply 'we hate humans!'[2] Now, Popper certainly does not write something like: I hate violent people, or: I hate those who hate humans, but he says that he hates violence – that is to say, precisely, an ideal term, or an ideality. The distinction between *ideas* or principles, especially if they are bad and should be eliminated, and *individuals* who adopt or believe in them, who should be respected as persons and, if possible, rescued from them, is a classical one which is always extremely useful. It has to do with the very conditions of Right and Justice. However, it is not always possible to *separate* individual humans from their ideals (in other times we might have said: from their soul or their spirits); above all, we may wonder whether there is not something which, precisely, is *intermediary* between ideas and individuals, sharing the nature of both, and rendering them inseparable: *groups, collectives bodies.*

As soon as *groups* come into the picture – and how can they *not* come into the picture, especially in the social and political realm? – the question really is whether 'hating violence' in order to eliminate its causes, and to reverse the violent tendencies in society with a view to defending human liberty and dignity, still comes down to hating something ideal, or has to imply also hating groups, institutions, forms of organization, collective bodies which *embody violence*, so to speak, and eliminating them. . . .

In a word, how do we 'eliminate the eliminators'?

What would be the alternative? Should it be 'non-violence'? Leaving aside for the moment the classical discussions about its effectiveness, let me suggest that even a quick reading of Freud might teach us that this is not necessarily the end of our dilemma, since non-violence may involve an effort to hate violence, or violent instincts, *within oneself,* and therefore something which can always border on self-destruction or desiring one's own death, even at a symbolic level – as if the alternative were between only two forms of destruction: *counter-violence* and *self-destruction* or *self-annihilation.* This, perhaps, is the moment to suggest that Popper is much more of a Platonist than he would admit himself, as probably is anyone who poses the ideality of law, communication, the human person, as an absolute, and an antidote to violence – anyone, that is, who thinks that violence can be fought by idealizing its negations, the various figures of non-violence: law, justice, love, respect. . . .

The second example I want to recall briefly is that of Georges Bataille – not all his work, that would be impossible, since in a sense it is devoted in its entirety to the question we are dealing with here, but one precise instance, which I isolate because it was frequently mentioned in debates around the alleged fascination of intellectuals, or some intellectuals, with violence.

In 1933–34 Bataille wrote a famous essay called 'La structure psychologique du fascisme',[3] in which he put forward an explanation or interpretation of fascism, and especially Nazism, in terms of the opposition between two aspects of social life: the 'homogeneous' – in short, the *order* or system of norms within which social conflicts themselves have to be maintained and organized if the structure of power and authority is to remain untouched – and the 'heterogeneous': infra-rational forces which are released as soon as the antagonism becomes irreconcilable, and can express themselves only in the form of violence. Although Bataille did not use the expression in his text, there was a clear association between these theoretical analyses and the political slogan which, at that time, Bataille and some of his friends coined in *Contre-Attaque,* the anti-fascist group of artists and intellectuals which he had created together with André Breton and other Surrealists. Bataille explained that a political movement of revolutionary intellectuals and workers who wanted to resist Nazism should not be properly *anti-fascist,* but '*sur-fasciste*', super-fascist – that is, should 'learn' something from fascism itself, rely upon the same violent, 'heterogeneous' forces that fascism was unleashing, and use them to destroy the capitalist order which the fascists were defending. This was one of the reasons which quickly led to a break between Bataille and André Breton, who, together with his own friends – some of whom joined the Communist Party – were supporting the Popular Front strategy.

Now, without going into the controversial debates about this story yet again, I would simply like to recall two facts.

One, contrary to some allegations, the majority of Sadeian–Nietzschean intellectuals in twentieth-century European history were not *fascists* (whereas some fascists were Nietzscheans, or believed to be so, and, to my knowledge, never Sadeians), but some of them came very near to believing that there is some truth in fascism, or that fascism can in some sense be fought only 'from the inside'.

Second, if something like a 'fascination of intellectuals for violence' exists, it is indeed bound up with a call for transgression, the transgression of certain prohibitions or interdictions. But among the interdictions that must be transgressed, there is not only the interdiction which outlaws rebellion in the name of law and order, forcing individuals to bow beneath the yoke of institutions and morality (remember Malebranche's incredible formula: 'The supreme virtue is the love of order'), but also the interdiction which prohibits knowing and investigating, a prohibition on knowing about violence in general and every particular instance of violence, as if there were a powerful interest keeping violence *outside* the realm of the knowable and the thinkable – or, better, outside the realm of what is thinkable as a 'normal' determination of social relations and a cause of political, social and historical effects. As if there were some sort of 'thought police' alongside the ordinary police on the street, who warn good citizens to keep away from a place where crimes or riots are taking place. Of course, the police do allow some 'experts' to study cases, applying statistical, sociological and psychological methods in order to make this or that form of individual or social violence an *object* of investigation and, possibly, control. But is this not precisely why some intellectuals, again, are tempted to transgress the interdiction – possibly we have all felt this temptation at one time or another – and also why some of them imagine that *nothing* – at least, nothing decisive – can really be thought *outside violence*, if thinking or writing does not itself become 'violent', or *model itself* on a certain violence?

Let me now look at the problem from a more substantial angle. We can begin with the classical dilemma concerning the uses and ambiguous meaning of the German term *Gewalt*, which *we*, according to circumstances, would translate as *violence, power* or *force*, or admit that it is untranslatable. . . . Derrida – following in the footsteps of others such as Marx, Weber, Benjamin, and Raymond Aron – discussed this question in *Force of Law*, setting up the stakes of the argument very clearly. I will take up this theme, but with two caveats.

First, I consider it to be basically equivalent to the question of the relations of force which are internal and external with respect to the institutions of apparatuses of historical *hegemony*, in a broader Gramscian sense. These institutions or apparatuses are *legitimate* by definition, even if they are not always capable of imposing their legitimacy. Let us note, in passing, that the idea of a legitimate power of *Gewalt* that is absolutely recognized, and therefore automatically implemented, is a contradition in terms. . . . The legitimacy of such apparatuses is of necessity dependent on that of great idealities, great transcendent *forms* in the Platonic sense, which, in turn, idealize their functioning. To name just a few: God and the State, or God and the Nation, or the Law itself (as *Torah, Nomos, Chariah* or *the Constitution*). (Is it an advantage or not that English does not, like French, distinguish between *loi* and *droit* – or, better, does not make the distinction between *law* and *right* in the same way?)

This, for the present purpose, would be my way of reformulating Althusser's thesis that state institutions are 'Ideological State Apparatuses'. But in order to designate this *nexus* of power, violence and ideality, I am even more inclined to borrow Hegel's notion of (objective) *Spirit*, used in his *Philosophy of Right* and *Philosophy of History*. Many of the questions that we have to confront here are already included in the Hegelian theory of history and the constitution of the state, inasmuch precisely as it is a theory of the objective Spirit – especially if we try to remain on the edge, so to speak, of the contradictions designated by this term, which is redolent of the hegemonic functioning of the State (and Religion) itself.

My second caveat: no reflection on social and historical violence can ever be circumscribed by questions of *power*, even decentred and decentralized power. This is precisely what the polysemy of the word *Gewalt* in German can help us to express, since it already goes beyond the limits of 'power'. The questions of power really lie at the heart of what I have called the economy of violence, inasmuch as there is a primary violence to power, and a counter-violence against power, or an attempt at building a counter-violence which takes the form of counter-violence. But there are layers of violence which do not gravitate around the alternative of power versus counter-power, although they inevitably return in them – *infect them*, so to speak (pathological metaphors are difficult to avoid here, since the very representation of power has to do with a certain concept of normality). This, if you like, is the most 'excessive', the most 'self-destructive' part of violence. Again, it is by no means certain that this is not a tautological discourse: we say that a certain kind of violence is *self-destructive* or *irrational*, because we feel that it eludes the logic of power and counter-power (I remember that such terms were used, for example, in the context of the so-called 'extreme forms' taken by the riots in Los Angeles when I happened to be there, immediately after the first Rodney King trial in 1993). Sometimes we use such terms to reassure ourselves, sometimes also in order to idealize violence in turn – for example, by using the term *sacrifice*, to which I will return.

I would say, against Foucault (or rather, against an idea that we have been all too eager to find in Foucault), that *there is power*, even a power apparatus, which has several centres, however complex and multiple these 'centres' may be. Indeed, power is never simple, neither is it stabilized and located for ever here or there, in these hands or those hands, in the form of this or that 'monopoly', but it is always *complexity-reducing*, as some sociologists would say, and it can reduce complexity, and therefore diversity (already a fairly violent process in some cases), not only by virtue of its material force, which would never suffice, or could never be sufficiently focused, but by virtue of its own transcedence. I would say: by virtue of the 'tautological power' and violence of its own *ideality*, as expressed in such formulas as *God is God, the Law is the Law*, which try to encapsulate the Absolute.[4] But, having said this, I shall parody Lacan and add: power cannot be all; in fact in essence it is 'not-all' [*pas-tout*], that is, deficient – even if we include in it its opposite and adversary, counter-power, that is, revolution and rebellion, 'anti-systemic movements', and so on.

To clarify – still on an abstract level – let me suggest that in order to cope with this inadequancy of the dialectic of power (or *Gewalt*, or *Spirit*, or domination), we need a third term. We cannot think in terms of simple antitheses like force and violence, or power and violence. What should this third term be?

Any choice of terminology is partly conventional. I might have thought of *barbarism*, but I shall avoid it, because this term has very precise ethnocentric connotations which derive from its opposition to civility and civilization. In fact we use this term because we believe that 'barbarians' exist (or have existed), and could return (*Ultimi barbarorum*, Spinoza once wanted to engrave on the walls of his city). I prefer – again with some arbitrariness – to use the word *cruelty*, and I shall argue that a phenomenology of violence has to deal, at the same time, with the intrinsic relationship between violence and power (expressed in the term *Gewalt*) and the intrinsic relationship between violence and cruelty, which is something else.

The phenomenology of power implies a 'spiritual' dialectic of power and counter-power, state and revolution, orthodoxy and heresy, which, throughout its development is composed of violent deeds and relations of violence. But it also includes – not beyond or apart from this development, but permanently intertwined with it – a demonstration of cruelty, which is *another* reality, like the emergence or glimpse of another scene. Although an essential part of the question is to understand why power itself, be it state power, colonial domination, male domination, and so on, has to be not only violent or powerful or brutal, but also cruel – why it has to derive from itself, and obtain from those who wield it, *jouissance* ('enjoyment')[5] – it seems to me that the key issue is that, contrary to what happens in the dialectics of the Spirit, there is nothing like a *centre*, not even a decentred centre, in cruelty.

I would say – borrowing Bataille's term – that there is something intrinsically *heterogeneous* in cruelty. Therefore it must have a quite different relationship to ideality, which does not mean that it has none. We could perhaps suggest that the violence-of-power, the *Gewalt*, has an immediate relationship with historical ideality and idealities, because, while it serves some very precise public and private *interests*, it never ceases to embody idealities, to implement them, to constitute itself as *the force* which crushes all resistance in order to embody idealities or ideal principles: God, the Nation, the Market. . . . The forms of cruelty, on the other hand, have a relationship with materiality which is *not mediated* (especially not symbolically mediated), although in this immediate relationship with materiality some terrible idealities *return*, so to speak, or become displayed and exhibited as *fetishes* and *emblems*.

This could be connected with the fact that in every process of symbolization of the materiality of history (which produces the very possibility of a representation of history – the state and revolution are highly symbolic in this respect), there is always a *residue*[6] of materiality. Now why this residue emerges mainly in the form of cruelty, or why it has to emerge in the form of cruelty, is extremely awkward, I admit, for anyone who is not inclined to embark on a discussion of *evil* because, among other reasons, he or she is not inclined to embark on a discussion of *Good* and *Goodness*. . . .

There is, of course, no question of discussing in detail the dialectic of power and its 'residue' of cruelty. What I would like to do, in the time which is left to me, is simply the following: first, to enumerate a number of classical questions – or, if you prefer, moments – which I think should feature in any presentation of this dialectic. And second, to go back to the enigmas of cruelty, and say a few things about why it seems to me that we are now confronting them in a way which is anything but marginal.

A dialectic of *Gewalt* (or the violence-of-power) should begin with the question of the *Law*, including its two aspects: the violent force of law and codified violence, or legitimate violence, or the right to exercise violence. On the one hand, the traditional antinomy which results from the fact that state power has a monopoly of violence and weapons (albeit not all of them, and not everywhere . . .) – in short, from the fact that the state *removes* violence and the means of violence from 'society' by taking them *for itself* and *upon itself*. The meaning and forms of this antinomy – of its theological and political mysteries, and so on – have been discussed from Hobbes to Kant, from Weber to Derrida. But there is also the other, more daily and profane aspect, codified violence: the violence of suppression, punishment, ancient and modern slavery, and so forth. Whenever we study concrete examples – the functioning of prisons, for instance – we discover that it proves extremely difficult to draw a clear line of demarcation *within* the realm of law itself – not a totalitarian juridical system, but the 'normal' civilized and liberal system – between *justice* and *violence*. And basically, I think, that if the so-called 'foundational violence' of state power is to exist (or appear as foundational), it must not only be idealized or sacralized – that goes without saying – but also *actually exercised* and implemented at *some points* and times, in some visible 'zones' of the system. . . . Hence the importance and difficulty of the problem of the death penalty, for instance. But here we realize that, in many cases, we are at the extreme borders of cruelty. And I hope it is not a mere play on words if I say that we also encounter the question of *borders* in general: social and territorial borders are privileged places where codified violence borders on cruelty. . . .

A dialectics of violence should go on to reflect on the fact that the permanent confrontation between power(s) and counter-power(s) does not imply only the periodic unleashing of violence and counter-violence, whose effectiveness partly depends on how powerfully it is symbolized and justified – on whether it contains a 'sublime' element. But there is a supplementary twist. In fact it seems to me – and the more I hear historians, philosophers, lawyers and political theorists discussing violence, the more I become convinced of it – that the fundamental – possibly the only logical and rhetorical – *schema* for the *legitimation* of violence is the schema of *preventive counter-violence.*

Any violence, in the sense of *Gewalt*, that has to become legally or morally legitimate must present itself if not as retaliation, at least as correction and suppression of *violent forces* – whether they be rooted in human nature, social conditions, or ideological beliefs – which have destroyed or disturbed an originary ideal, originally peaceful, non-violent order, or threaten it with destruction.

This schema can be applied either directly, in positivistic legal terms, immediately combining description with prescription, or referred back to some mythical or transcendental archetype which already tells the story of how Good and Evil, order and disorder, justice and violence, and so on, have conducted their eternal conflict. Of course, the state itself, or spiritual power, can appear, or be portrayed, as a violent disruptive force in this sense – the most violent and most disruptive of all. Hence the possibility of infinite mirror-games between 'society' (or 'civil society') and 'state', in which terms such as illegality, rebellion, revolution, and so forth, will feature.

But this is the main conclusion I would like to draw: if, at a fundamental institutional level, violence can be justified only as preventive counter-violence, then something called violence, or violent behaviour – be it public or private, individual or collective – will exist only inasmuch as its violent suppression is already antici-pated. In other words what we call 'violence' and the lines of demarcation we draw between what is supposed to be violent behaviour and what is not, will exist only retrospectively, in the anticipated recurrence of counter-violence. And this has direct effects on the analysis of violence, or research into its manifestations and causes.

A power which organizes itself as preventive counter-violence undoubtedly needs certain information about violence: juridical classifications, sociological and psychological explanations and pre-dictions, statistical records of its progression or regression, and so on. Without this, there would be no police and no politics. But the suspicion will never be eliminated – at least for those who contribute professionally to this knowledge – that there must be a basic element of *misrecognition,* a blind spot, in the midst of this ever-expanding knowledge, which stems from the fact that this knowledge is not only associated with power – as is all knowledge – but, more precisely, produced under the schema of preventive counter-violence, or the *re-establishment of order.* Here, indeed, a careful discussion of Foucault's epistemological investigation into the productivity of power is unavoidable.

Finally, I think that a dialectics of *Gewalt* must include a description of the most idealistic, the most spiritual and apparently 'soft' forms of violence which are connected with the history of power. In a recent text on the history of state institutions, Pierre Bourdieu quotes a passage from one of Thomas Bernhardt's novels where he equates education with violence – more precisely, with state violence.[7] This is because any basic process of education, which aims not only at normalizing subjects, but also at *making* them bearers of the values and ideals of society, or at integrating them into the fabric of 'hegemony' – as I have called it, following Gramsci – mainly by means of *intellectual* processes, is not mere *learning,* an acquisition of capacities, knowledge, ideas, and so on, written on a *tabula rasa,* as classical empiricist liberalism innocently imagined. On the contrary, it has to be a deconstruction of an already existing identity and a reconstruction of a new one.

I would go so far as to say: it has to be a *dis-membering* in order to become a *re-membering* or recasting of the mind – which inevitably confers on the mind a mode of existence which is akin to that of a body. One could put it in religious terms: all education is a 'conversion'. And there is a long story to be written here, taking into account continuities and differences: beginning for instance, with the *compelle eos intrare* of Saint Luke and Saint Augustine (we all know that although this lent itself to military applications, it basically had a spiritual meaning), and going on to the crises of the modern school system, in both its 'authoritarian' and its 'libertarian' forms. Sometimes the libertarian forms are *the most violent,* because they put the burden of dis-membering and re-membering upon the child him- or herself, thereby asking him or her to be his or her own surgeon and engineer and torturer, the *heautontimoroumenos*.

And here, again, we have to investigate how the dialectic of *Gewalt*, violent and ideality, *borders on cruelty*, or always hangs over abysses of cruelty, both noticed and unnoticed. And since I have been quoting Bourdieu, I might as well add that the very situation which he initially described as the most favourable one in terms of education success – the situation of the bourgeois 'inheritors', those who have already absorbed from their family setting the linguistic, literary and moral skills and customs which the school will expect from them, or the so-called 'pre-knowledge' for these skills – might very well be the most ambivalent of all. No doubt it is socially rewarding, but it can prove less 'protective' in terms of internal negotitions with the ferocity of the superego. This might explain – if it is true – why kids from the working classes, the popular classes, either reject the school system (or are rejected by it) or improve their social status through that system, but are seldom psychologically destroyed by it – bearing in mind, of course, that there are more directly economic factors.

Now let me go back to cruelty, and finish with a few words about why, as I said, I consider the question especially relevant nowadays. First of all, I should confess that I am by no means certain that the phenomena I am thinking of have any real unity. They are clearly heterogeneous, and we had better not try to impose upon them some sort of common essence which would be only metaphysical – such as, precisely, *evil*. On the other hand, I suspect that this heterogeneity is intrinsic to the very way cruelty can be displayed in experience or history. Let me mention two kinds of phenomena.

First, some typical aspects fo what I would call the *internal exclusion of the poor* in our societies (so-called 'affluent' societies), sometimes referred to as the 'new poverty'. Why is this situation so hopeless?

I am fully aware of the fact that the element of cruelty, or the 'border' of cruelty, was never absent from classical forms of the exploitation of labour and unemployment. This reminds us of the fact (for which Marx provided a fairly convincing explanation) that the capitalist economy is based not only upon exploitation, but upon an *excess of exploitation* , or *super-exploitation* – this is something we have sometimes tended to forget. I am also mindful of the fact that the most massive form of poverty in today's world is the one we see in *underdeveloped* countries, where the combination of the destruction of traditional activities, the domination of foreign financial institutions, the establishment of a so-called New World Order, and so on, leads to a situation – which, of course, nobody either wanted or anticipated – in which millions of human beings are *superfluous*. Nobody needs them – they are, so to speak, disposable people – to borrow the extremely violent expression which Bertrand Ogilvie proposed at a conference in Montevideo.[8] So, they are facing – and we are facing once more – the prospect of an extermination whose forms are not only violent but specifically *cruel* – I am thinking, for example, of the half-voluntary, half-involuntary; half-conscious, half-unconscious forms in which AIDS has been spreading through Africa right from the beginning.

But even if 'the North' is not experiencing this kind of situation, the advent of the 'new poverty', or the 'underclass' of the unemployed, could be called cruel or, at the very least, extremely undesirable. The second or third generation of young unemployed people does not, by definition, *predate* the establishment of a social (welfare) state, more or less complete legal rules of social security; they *come after* its partial failure and dismembering. Hence we have a 'post-historical' situation, a double-bind which Marx could not have anticipated, since he thought that unemployment was a cyclical phenomenon, a provisional stage used by capital to lower the wage level in the course of a continuous expansion. Now, provisional or not, the situation is that millions of disposable human beings are at the same time excluded from labour – that is, *economic activity* – and kept within the boundaries of the *market*, since the market is an absolute; it has no *external limits*. The Market is the World. When it excludes you, you cannot leave it, search for another America, settle there and start again. . . .

A second form of cruelty is warfare, and particularly those so-called 'ethnic' and 'religious' wars, with their apparent irrationality, which have reintroduced the concept of genocide or extermination in the post-Cold War world, both North and South, under the name of 'ethnic cleansing'. (To interpose a personal anecdote: I am slightly disturbed by the fact that I myself met with one of the future theoreticians of ethnic cleansing some years ago in America, since he kindly agreed to be my interlocutor after a lecture I gave at Boston University.) The very fact that ethnic cleansing is not only *practised* but also *theorized* – that again and again, the violence of extermination appears as a passage *à l'acte*, becomes implemented as an 'acting out' of a theoretical script which is also obviously fantasmatic (albeit deeply rooted in the substratum of the nation-state and the nation-form) – could be considered, I think, to be the imprint of an outbreak of cruelty – that is, a violence which is not completely intelligible in the logic of power or the economy of *Gewalt*.

I deliberately mentioned the enigmatic and indirect relationship between underdevelopment, so-called overpopulation, and the spread of AIDS in Africa, because we can introduce here a kind of tentative and uncertain symmetry. The 'disposable human being' is indeed a social phenomenon, but it tends to look, at least in some cases, like a 'natural' phenomenon, or a phenomenon of violence in which the boundaries between what is human and what is natural, or what is post-human and what is post-natural, tend to become blurred: what I would be tempted to call an *ultra-objective* form of violence, or *cruelty without a face*; whereas the practices and theories of ethnic cleansing confront us with what I would call *ultra-subjective* forms of violence, or *cruelty with a Medusa face*. This, of course, is related to the fact that they unleash and realize 'in the Real', at a collective level, processes which are not, and cannot be, completely symbolized, which in Freudian terms would be described as primary or pre-Oedipal.

I am not necessarily taking on board all the theorization that goes along with these terms; I use them for their descriptive power. And this power, of course, is attributable to the fact that in such situations – witness collective rapes in Yugoslavia or in India or elsewhere – social violence becomes heavily sexualized. In other words, the 'normally' sexualized character of social practices in modern societies crosses a certain threshold, and the limits between the individual and the collective, the real and the imaginary, become blurred. This was indeed already the case with Nazism, and other totalitarian phenomena in history; therefore a careful comparative examination is required, including both massive and local, 'exceptional' and 'ordinary' practics. I cannot but think here of the terrible tale written by the Spanish writer Rafael Sanchez Ferlosio, for the 500th anniversary of the so-called 'discovery of America', in which he describes how the Spanish *conquistadores* used their dogs of war, for which they had invented noble names and genealogies, in the hunting of American Indians.[9] Indeed, there is no basic difference between this form of cruelty and the similarly ritualized forms displayed by the SS in Nazism. A difference arose in the end, however, from the fact that the *conquistadores* were acting in the framework of an extremely powerful *hegemony* – under the authority of an extremely powerful *ideality*, namely the Catholic religion, combining legal apparatus and messianic faith, which allowed them to subsume the practices of cruelty under the discourses of hegemony – that is, a spiritual and material violence which could be disciplined and 'civilized'.

I offer no conclusion, simply some final remarks and questions: (1) how can we imagine that current forms of cruelty in today's world can be contained by new institutions, which, one way or another, will continue the dialectics of *Gewalt*, be they state institutions or revolutionary institutions? (2) supposing – which I would be ready to admit – that the counterpart to the experience of cruelty is always some sort of particularly demanding thirst for *ideality* – either in the sense of *non-violent* ideals, or in the sense of ideals of *justice* – how are we to deal philosophically and practically with what I consider to be a matter of incontrovertible finality: that there is no liberation from violence, no resistance to its worst excesses, especially no *collective* resistance (but a resistance that is not collective can hardly be called a resistance) *without ideals*? However, there is no guarantee, and there can be no guarantee, concerning the 'good use' and the 'bad use' of ideals – or, if you prefer, there are certainly *degrees* in the amount of violence which goes along with civilizing ideals; but nothing like a *zero* degree. Therefore there is no such thing as non-violence. This we should bear in mind, I think, while we struggle against excessive violence in all its many forms.

Notes

1. Lecture delivered at The Society for the Humanities, Cornell University, Ithaca, 24 February 1995. The amended and expanded French version was published as 'Violence: idéalité et cruauté' in Étienne Balibar, *La Crainte des masses: Politique et philosophie avant et après Marx* (Paris: Galilée, 1997).

2. Papers from the Centre for New Ethnicities Research, University of East London.

3. See Georges Bataille, *Oeuvres complètes*, (Paris: Éditions de Minuit, 1970), vol. 1, pp. 339–71.

4. On the ambivalent effects of such 'tautological' formulas, see Stanislas Breton, '*Dieu est Dieu*: Essai sur la violence des propositions tautologiques', in *Philosophie buissonnière* (Grenoble: Jérôme Millon, 1989).

5. See Slavoj Žižek, *The Metastases of Enjoyment: Six Essays on Women and Causality* (London and New York: Verso 1994).

6. See Jean-Jacques Lecercle, *The Violence of Language* (London and New York: Routledge, 1990).

7. The novel is *Ancient Masters*. See Pierre Bourdieu, 'L'État et la concentration du capital symbolique', in B. Théret *et al.*, *L'État, la finance et le social* (Paris: La Découverte, 1993), p. 73.

8. See Bertrand Ogilvie, 'Violence et représentation: La production de l'homme jetable', paper presented at the *Violencia y traumatismos historicos* Conference, Montevideo 1994, reprinted in *Lignes*, 26, October 1995.

9. See the French translation: 'Lâchez les chiens! Prélude au 500ᵉ anniversaire de la découverte des Amériques', *Les Temps Modernes*, 509, December 1988.

8

Ambiguous Universality

I have entitled this contribution 'Ambiguous Universality' because I intend to show that no discussion about universality (and, consequently, no discussion about its contraries or opposites: particularity, difference, singularity) can usefully proceed with a 'univocal' concept of 'the universal'. Such a discussion has to take into account the concept's insurmountable *equivocity*. In a sense, this is a commonplace, which every great philosophy has tried to clarify, but also to reduce, notably by integrating modes or modalities of the universal within a single dialectical progression: just think of Hegel's schema of integration of juridical ('abstract' or 'formal') universality within moral (or 'subjective') universality, itself integrated within 'ethical' or 'concrete' (i.e. social and historical) universality, to become finally a moment in the realization of 'the Absolute'. Our experience with thinking and building institutions has been, however, that such integrative patterns are not able to 'reconcile' or completely 'mediate' the conflicting concepts and experiences of universality. This situation does not seem to me to imply that we should give up the notion of universality, or view it as a mystification or an 'idol', or try to establish instead one of its opposites in the position of a 'Master Word' of philosophy (such as the Singular, or Difference, or the Particular). Rather, I shall argue that it should lead us to accept the scattered meaning of the universal, and elaborate the passages between its different modalities. The philosophical project would thus become to articulate these differences, to seek an 'intelligible order' between them – which is always, in the last instance, a matter of ethical and political choice rather than pure speculative or theoretical construction.

In the following pages, I shall gather my remarks around three successive points of view on the question of universality: *universality as 'reality'* which, as we shall see, leads to questioning again the representations of unity and diversity; *universality as 'fiction'*, which seems to me the right way to discuss the institutional combinations of seeming 'opposites', such as universalism and particularism; finally, *universality as a 'symbol'* which, for reasons that I shall explain later, I would also call 'ideal universality'. My terminology is a tentative one; it could be transformed if other terms prove clearer or more accurate. It has also to take into account the fact that each of these 'moments' is itself, in many respects, a contradictory one.

Universality as Reality

Let us start with *real* universality. I take it in the sense of an actual interdependency between the various 'units' which, together, build what we call *the world*: institutions, groups, individuals, but also, more profoundly, the various *processes* which involve institutions, groups and individuals: the circulation of commodities and people, the political negotiations, the juridical contracts, the communication of news and cultural patterns, and so on.

This interdependency has an *extensive* aspect: the 'limits' or 'extremities of the world' have now been reached by various modes of exploration, or the expansion of dominant, unified technologies and institutions have incorporated 'all parts of the world'. It has above all an *intensive* aspect: more aspects of the life of the constitutive units are dependent on what other units have been doing in the past, or are currently doing. Another – perhaps more concrete – formulation for this intensive aspect could be expressed by saying that interdependence is *reaching the individual himself or herself* in a *direct* manner, not only through the institutions or communities to which he or she belongs. Of course, the extensive and intensive aspects are interdependent. It is the extensive aspect which is concerned when colonization included all inhabited territories, when the world is actually divided into nation-states belonging to the single 'United Nations Organization', or communication networks can broadcast the same programmes everywhere. It is the intensive aspect which is concerned when every individual's wage and skill become dependent on competitors anywhere on the world market, but also when educational curricula must include the learning of international languages, or sanitary regulations must control the individual's food and sexual habits because of the spread of world epidemics (AIDS).

Many readers will say: 'real' universality in this sense is nothing really new. It did not always exist, to be sure: there was a time when 'the world' as an entity was not conceivable, except in physical or cosmological terms. But it has existed at least since the emergence of the 'modern world'; therefore it has been the permanent background of what we call modernity. This is certainly true. I will therefore make my point more clearly. There have been stages in the extension and intensification of real universality, until 'in the end', a decisive *threshold* was crossed, which made it irreversible (we might also say: which makes it impossible to achieve any proper 'delinking', or to imagine any return to 'autarky' within the world system); and a moment has also come when *utopian* figures of universality have become obsolete by their very nature. By utopian figures I mean any intellectual plans of establishing universality by connecting humankind with itself, creating a 'cosmopolis' – which was always imagined at the same time as an implementation of certain moral values, precisely 'universalistic' values. This impossibility did not arise because it proved impossible to connect the world as a single space, but exactly for the opposite reason: because this connection of humankind with itself was already achieved, because it was *behind us*. The two aspects are therefore bound together, as a matter of fact. But this fact is acknowledged belatedly and reluctantly. Why? Perhaps because, though it does not mark the 'end of history', it nevertheless marks the practical end of 'cosmopolitical' utopias, because it involves acknowledging that real universality, or globalization, already achieves the goal which was conceived as 'the unification of mankind', albeit certainly without implementing most of the moral (or 'humanistic') values which utopias represented as either a precondition or an immediate consequence of this unification.

In other terms, we could say that it is no longer a question of *creating* 'the (true) world', or the 'unity of the world', but of *transforming* it from within. It is no accident if we are reminded here of a celebrated phrase from Marx's *Theses on Feuerbach*: 'The philosophers have only *interpreted* the world, in various ways; the point is to *change* it.' A world which has to be transformed is an 'actually existing' world, a real universality. No doubt Marx had an acute perception that real universality was well on its way towards realization, which he associated with the establishment of a single 'division of labour' and a process of 'commodification' of all social relations. At the same time, however, he associated this idea with a 'radical simplification' of social structures, a withering away of traditional forms of domination which, he thought, would be reduced to the pure exploitation of wage labour, leading to the final antagonism of individuality and capitalism all over the world, and hence towards a 'catastrophic' overcoming of alienation in communisim, or a reconciliation of man with himself. This, perhaps, is the paradoxical figure of Marx: the last utopian announcing the end of the very possibility of utopias.

But real universality in today's world is by no means restricted to the global expansion of economic structures. It has also become political (with the progressive emergence of transnational strategies, of political 'subjects' irreducible to local agencies, based on a single territory), and cultural and communicative (with dominant networks and countercultural initiatives dialectically interacting across traditional borders). As a consequence, the analytical schema that seems best adapted to interpreting the expressions of this world-politics is the Hobbesian one of a 'war of all against all', rather than a Marxian–Hegelian schema of growing antagonism between symmetrical forces. The Hobbesian schema, however, reaches its limits when it is a question of getting to the next step: namely, the possibility of controlling the conflictual elements by settling above them some juridical and political single authority, be it through coercion or general consent. A 'world Leviathan', or a world-scale 'rational-central rule', seems incompatible with the complexity we are facing: new modes of regulation are needed if we are not to be doomed to an eternal 'Behemoth'.

Let me now add some remarks about the figure of the 'complex world system' in this sense. The geographical and geopolitical pattern of the world has been subjected to considerable modifications. The very term 'globalization' still reminds us of a process in which it was the 'centre' (in fact made up of rival powers) which was incorporating successive 'peripheries' and outer regions (Wallerstein's 'external arenas') within the limits of its domination. This process took the form of subjecting states and societies, importing goods and men, exploiting manpower and natural resources, exporting languages, techniques, and institutions (ultimately the nation-state itself). What we are now experiencing is the 'backlash' effect of this process. It is not the suppression of domination and economic inequalities (perhaps it could be said that the polarization of wealth and misery, power and dependency, has reached unprecedented levels) but the multiplication of centres, forming a network rather than a 'core' area. And it is the reverse movement which projects elements of the former periphery into the 'central' societies.

Above all, the phenomenon of transnational migrations acquires a new quality. It is here, particularly, that a precise historical analysis is required in order to avoid simplistic 'Eurocentric' or 'Western' prejudices. As the Mexican sociologist Pablo Gonzalez Casanova remarked at a recent conference in Paris, colonial and 'Third World' countries have long experienced what we in the 'North' now call *multiculturalism*. Far from being 'backward' in this respect, they were showing the way. It becomes clear that this highly conflictual and also evolutionary pattern was not a transitory one, a provisional (albeit massive) 'exception' on the road to modernization (mainly conceived as 'westernization'): it is the general situation in the era of real universality.[1] Whether or not this will be compatible with the simple continuation of the political and cultural forms which had emerged with European (and North American) hegemony, notably the (more or less completely sovereign) nation-state and (more or less unified) national culture, is exactly what is at stake in current debates on 'the New World Order', on dominant and dominated languages, religious and literary standards in education, and so on.

I would like to emphasize the latent transformation which the notion of *minority* is undergoing in this situation. 'Minority' is a complex notion which refers to either a juridical or a sociopolitical realm.

Juridically speaking, 'minors' are those human individuals and groups who are subjected to the more or less 'protective' authority of full citizens: the classic example being that of children with respect to their parents. It is mainly in this sense that Immanuel Kant, in a famous text, defined the global process of emancipation of humankind which he called *Aufkärung* as 'man's emergence from his self-incurred immaturity'. Clearly, other groups have long been maintained in a minority status: women, servants, colonized peoples, and 'coloured' people in racial states (not to mention slaves), and there is no doubt that, in spite of winning formal equality one after the other, none of them has totally achieved complete equality, or *parity*, in terms of rights and duties, access to responsibilities, social prestige, and so forth.

The other meaning is more a question of administration and statistics: it refers to the fact that religious and/or ethnic groups are living among a 'majoritarian' population – usually in the framework of some national or imperial state – where they are segregated, or subjected to some special legislation, or protected, but also where their collective 'identity' is threatened with assimiliation to the majoritarian – that is, dominant – identity. Here I would like to emphasize the following fact. By definition, 'minority' in this sense, whether or not it was associated with a status of juridical minority, was considered an *exceptional* phenomenon. More precisely, it was a *normalized exception*. Nineteenth-century nationalism and nation-building politics had led to a double-edged situation. On the one hand, it was considered 'normal' that a nation-state be 'ethnically' (if not religiously) homogeneous, above all from the point of view of the official language (which had all sorts of cultural effects, since it was the language of law, politics, education, administration, etc.). On the other hand, it was precisely because political entities wre generally conceived of as nation-states that minorities officially existed – that is to say, populations were formally classified according to their 'national' or 'ethnic' (sometimes also religious) membership, and individuals were identified with their 'common' majoritarian or minoritarian status, in spite of all their other differences and likenesses. The very existence of minorities, together with their more or less inferior status, *was a state contruct*, a strict correlate of the nation-form.

Real universality produces a very ambivalent effect on this situation. It *generalizes minority status*, first of all in the sense that there are now 'minorities' everywhere, be they of ancient or recent origin – not only of local descent, but from virtually all over the world. However, *the distinction between 'minorities' and 'majorities' becomes blurred* in a number of ways. First of all, it is blurred because a growing number of individuals and groups are not easily inscribed in one single ethnic (or cultural, linguistic, even religious) identity. I emphasize this point, which is highly sensitive politically. 'Communitarian' discourse (including the extreme form claiming 'ethnic purity'), which can arise from both dominant and dominated groups, mainly emphasizes the fact that societies have become more heterogeneous – that there are more and more 'others' permanently settled among the 'national' population: more 'Hispanic' people who are not likely simply to adopt the dominant 'Anglo-Saxon' culture in the US; more 'Islamic' people who are not likely to abandon or hide their languages and beliefs in Western Europe, and so on. But this is obviously only one side of the coin, the other side being that among these 'others', and among the 'nationals' as well (notably through intermarriage), *more and more individuals are not classifiable*: marrying partners from different 'cultures' and 'races,' living across the fictitious boundaries of communities, experiencing a divided or multiple 'self', experiencing different languages and memberships according to the private and public circumstances. These phenomena are anything but marginal. We might summarize them by saying that, as minorities proliferate, what 'minority' means becomes rather obscure – unless it is forcefully imposed: at very high human cost (as we observe today, tragically, in ex-Yugoslavia).

Another way of signalling this contradictory process refers to the effect of supra-national constructions, however precarious they may be. Take the case of Western Europe. In each nation-state you will find 'minorities' with respect to the 'majoritarian' population – although their definition is anything but standardized, because they are either linguistic or religious (or vaguely attributed to some traditional linguistic, religious, cultural differences); either settled on some specific territory or scattered throughout the country, either of ancient descent or recent settlement ('immigrants'); enjoying either full citizenship or the status of foreigners; coming either from neighbouring countries or from distant areas, and so on. Now, if you consider the global pattern from a *European* point of view, it may appear that the 'majorities' themselves are minorities, or that the linguistic, religious, cultural attributes that characterize them have no absolute privilege on the global stage. Even those populations which are represented politically by a strong state (English, French, German) are no longer absolute points of reference. At the same time, cultural characteristics which were 'minoritarian' in each nation-state – for example, the Muslim religious and cultural background – provide a common interest, and become potential links between populations of different origin within the emerging political entity of 'Europe'. It becomes difficult to give a rational justification for the fact that, among the various intertwining cultural groups which form the ethnic and social pattern of 'Europe' as a whole, contributing to its economic and cultural life, or to the functioning of its institutions, some enjoy a privileged status, while others are discriminated against. '*Apartheid*', which was hardly visible on the national stage, becomes apparent on the supra-national one: but these levels are becoming less and less distinct. Indeed, this is a situation which leads significant parts of the 'majoritarian' groups to feel threatened with reduction to a lower status, especially in a situation of economic crisis, where the 'national-social' (so-called welfare) state is partly dismantled. Openly or not, ideologies of 'ethnic cleansing', however arbitrary from the historical point of view, are likely to develop within national boundaries or at a continental level.

With all its narrowness and peculiarities, this pattern could be taken as a model of what is emerging on a world scale: *minorities without stable or unquestionable majorities*. It also draws our attention to the most explosive contradiction of real universality: the combination of ethnic differences and social inequalities within a global pattern of *internal exclusion*.

As a combined result of colonialism, imperial rule and national class struggles, a process of (at least partial) social integration, together with a dominant tendency towards cultural assimilation, had taken place within the boundaries of the more 'developed' nations of the 'core', while major status differences and acute social polarization were concentrated in the 'periphery'. To a large extent, socialist and anti-imperialist regimes had been attempts at filling this gap, fighting against 'external exclusion'. Now the simple division between developed and underdeveloped areas inherited from imperialism is blurred: economic polarization in the world system is less directly expressed in territorial structures; class diferences and ethnic discriminations are conjoined or overdetermined in a similar way in both North and South; 'internal exclusion' replaces external separations everywhere. Something like a world 'underclass' emerges, whereas, at the other extreme, a new transnational class of privileged rulers acquire common interests and language. This is undoubtedly one of the main reasons for the new outbreak of racism threatening to overwhelm humanistic values: always admitting – as I have argued elsewhere (Balibar and Wallerstein) – that racism is not a simple excess of identity feelings or xenophobia, but more specifically linked with internal exclusion, that is hostility and discrimination among populations which are not really separated, but belong to the *same* society and are culturally *mixed* with one another.

The immediate prospects may appear rather grim – not to mention the long-term resolution of the contradiction, which would require basic transformations of the social and economic structures. From a theoretical point of view, however, things could be summarized as follows: real universality is a stage in history where, for the first time, 'humankind' as a single web of interrelationships is no longer an ideal or utopian notion but an actual condition for every individual; nevertheless, far from representing a situation of mutual recognition, it actually coincides with a generalized pattern of conflicts, hierarchies and exclusions. It is not even a situation in which individuals communicate at least virtually with each other, but much more one where global communication networks provide every individual with a distorted image or a stereotype of all the others, either as 'kin' or as 'aliens', thus raising gigantic obstacles to any dialogue. 'Identities' are less isolated *and* more incompatible, less univocal *and* more antagonistic.

Universality as Fiction

Let us now examine a quite different concept, which I call *fictive universality*. Of course there is some degree of arbitrariness in any terminology. Misunderstandings can be avoided only in the progressive elaboration of the argument. When I say that universality should also be considered 'fictive', I am not suggesting that it does not exist, that it is a mere possibility, a ghost or an idea as opposed to the world of facts. *Ideal universality* will come later. The kind of 'fiction' I want to deal with has to do with very effective processes, above all *institutions* and *representations*: I take it, therefore, in the sense of 'constructed reality'. On the other hand, I want to avoid the common idea that every identity, be it personal or collective, could be considered a 'construct' in the same general sense, because this classical relativistic view – so it seems to me – leads to a levelling of the historical processes which create and hierarchize forms of identity and individuality, so that some of them become more 'basic' than others, and form a common background to their becoming complementary or incompatible. Such distinctions seem to me all the more necessary when the *normative* structures of identity and individuality, or the institutions which produce a common representation of 'what it means to be a person', to 'be oneself', or to be a 'subject', and the institutions which continuously enforce these representations upon human beings through education and social experience, are put into question: what is sometimes referred to as a 'crisis' of values. What is at stake is precisely the 'non-natural' but also 'non-arbitrary' character of subjective norms and patterns of individuality.

There is indeed a long tradition in the social sciences dealing with fictive universality in this sense. For my present purpose, however, I find a philosophical reference more useful: Hegel's construction of an 'ethical' notion of the individual (what he called *Sittlichkeit*). This is probably because Hegel, dependent as he was on a particular set of social values (those of the 'modern state' or the '*Rechtsstaat*' which found its 'rational' shape in Western Europe towards the end of the eighteenth and the beginning of the nineteenth century, after the 'bourgeois revolutions'), was acutely aware of the conflict, and therefore the analogies and incompatibilities, between *two conflicting realizations of universality*: the religious and the national-political. In a sense it could be said that Hegel's dialectic of history had no other object than precisely explaining how one great historical 'fiction', that of the universalistic church, could be substituted by another historical 'fiction', that of the secular, rational institutions of the state (in practice, the nation-state), with equally universalistic aims.

To be sure, Hegel's view of this process was associated with the idea that historical development necessarily leads from religious universality to political universality (in Hegelian terms, religious universality is 'rational' only *an sich*, or in alienated form, whereas political universality is 'rational' *für sich*, or consciously). In other words, he saw it as an irreversible *progress*. Therefore political universality, notwithstanding its fictive character, should appear as an absolute. What we are experiencing today is clearly a relativization of this view, which goes along with impressive phenomena of 'religious revival'. I would rather say: we are finding that political universality itself displays internal contradictions, while the contradictions of religion are still alive; or we are finding that the 'crisis' of religious hegemonies remains open to new developments, while the 'crisis' of the nation-form is already developing, with no predictable end. But this critique of Hegel's conception of linear progress does not negate the relevance of his analytical construction. In fact, on the contrary, what I have called 'fictive universality' could also be labelled 'Hegelian universality'.

What makes the Hegelian construction[2] so very relevant is the fact that it transcends any formal opposition between 'holism' and 'individualism'. What Hegel is concerned with is the intrinsic relationship between the construction of *hegemony*, or *total ideology*, and *autonomous individuality*, or *the person*. Both universalistic religions and national state-building rely upon 'total' ideologies, encompassing a number of different 'identities' and 'memberships'. They claim to represent universality as such, but they are opposed to 'totalitarian' world-views, where all individuals are supposed to adopt one and the same system of beliefs, or follow compulsory rules, for the sake of salvation and identification with some common essence. They are *pluralistic* by nature.[3] This amounts to saying that 'total' ideologies are intrinsically connected with the recognition (and before that, the institution) of the individual as a realtively autonomous entity: not one which is absolutely free from particular identities and memberships, but one which is never reducible to them, which ideally and also practically (in the day-to-day working of basic institutions, such as sacraments, marriage, courts, education, elections, etc.) *transcends* the limitations and qualifications of particular identities and memberships. This is precisely what should be understood as (fictive) *universality*: not the idea that the common nature of individuals is given or already there, but, rather, the fact that it is produced inasmuch as particular identities are relativized, and become mediations for the realization of a superior and more abstract goal.

What I want to show, therefore, by very schematically outlining a kind of Hegelian dialectic of hegemony, is both that this figure is very effective, and that it has a very strict prerequisite, which can lead to its crisis and internal collapse under other material conditions (notably economic ones). It is very effective because *individuality itself is always an institution*; it has to be represented and acknowledged; this can be achieved only if the individual is released from a strict membership or a 'fusion' within his or her *Gemeinschaft*, thus becoming able to adopt various social roles, to 'play' on several memberships, or to 'shift identity' in order to perform different social functions, while remaining a member of a superior community, or a 'subject'. It has its problematic prerequisites, however, because it is connected with the imposition of *normality*, a normal or standard way of life and set of beliefs (a 'dominant' practical ideology), which has to be maintained for successive generations – at least for the overwhelming majority, or the 'mainstream', across class and other barriers.

Universal religions achieved both results; this explains why they still provide 'ideal types' of hegemony. They did not suppress loyalties to the family, professional status, ethnic belongings and racial differences, social and political hierarchies, and so on. On the contrary – with the exception of 'apocalyptic' movements and crises – they depicted absolute reciprocity among the faithful, or perfect love of one's neighbour, as a transcendent goal, which could be reached only after death (or after the Last Judgement): a matter of hope, not of political strategy. But they urged individuals to live their particular lives internally (and, as much as possible, externally) according to the transcendent goal of salvation, or – to put it better – according to rules which were supposed to fit this ideal. This set up the symbolic framework which allowed particular institutions to become 'Christian' (or 'Islamic') institutions, to be lived and represented as *indirect means* or mediations towards final salvation. Thus particular institutions, communities and reciprocities were re-established or transformed, but always integrated within a totality. An individual could be recognized as a member of his or her various communities (family, profession, neighbourhood); he or she could act according to their obligations or enjoy their privileges or *support* their burdens – as a father or a mother, a soldier or a priest, a master or a servant, a Frenchman or a German, and so on – inasmuch as his or her various practices were sacralized or sanctified, and there were particular rites for all the corresponding circumstances. But the reverse was also true: any of these qualifications and practices, whether distributed among different social groups or successively performed by the same individuals, could be experienced as intrinsic mediations of the religious life.

The same is true for national hegemony, wherever it was achieved in the form of building an independent state which succeeded in 'nationalizing' the main aspects of social life and culture: this is the most concrete meaning we can give to the notion of *secularization*. From a religious point of view, national hegemony is often seen as pure uniformization, if not as totalitarian; just as, from a secular national point of view, religious hegemony is seen as incompatible with individual autonomy. Indeed, both hegemonies have different views of what is essential to human personality. They also have different, symmetrical, *points d'honneur* which are supposed to reveal the supreme value which they try to create. In the case of universal religions, the *point d'honneur* is peace among nations, the recognition of a supra-national community by all political powers. In the case of the nation-state, it is, rather, peace or tolerance among the various religious dominations (and more generally, on this model: the various ideologies), in the name of citizenship and legal order. In fact, both are *pluralistic* from their *own* point of view, that is, within their own *limits*. Nation-states adopt various means (according to their particular history, which is generally conflict-ridden and bloody) to make peace among religions, regional identities or ethnic memberships, and class loyalties.[4] Usually these means have nothing to do with real or strict equality; they are permeated with relations of force, but they are successful inasmuch as they allow particular communities and networks not only to become integrated in the 'total community' (national citizenship), but, much more, to work as its mediations. *Recognized differences*, or otherness-within-the-limits-of-citizenship, become the essential mediation of national membership.

Of course, you could wonder why I have called this mechanism 'universality'. Or you could say: it is universal only because of its 'false consciousness', because a Church or a State, as an institution of power needs a legitimizing discourse in which its own peculiarity or one-sidedness is masked and transfigured through the representation of 'ideological' goals and values. This aspect undoubtedly exists. It was emphasized by the Marxist critique, and it is revived whenever a 'radical' discourse criticizes the state, the school system, the legal system, and so forth, viewing them as so many means of domination in the service of a ruling class or group (be it the group of capitalists, or imperialists, or white men, or males, and so on). But it can work, and create a 'consensus' or a 'hegemony', only because it is rooted in a more elementary structure, which is *truly* universalistic. I think that such a structure always exists when a second-order community – or a 'Terminal Court of Appeal', as

Ernest Gellner calls it – is raised above 'traditional' or 'natural' or 'primary' memberships, addressing their members *qua* individuals – that is, whenever immediate memberships are virtually deconstructed and reconstructed as organic parts of the whole. Seen from outside (from the 'absolute' standpoint of world history), totality itself can certainly appear to be highly *particularistic*: there are *several* 'universal religions', or rival interpretations of religious universality, just as there are *several* nation-states and nationalist ideologies, each of them claiming to embody universal values (each claiming, one way or another, to be the 'elect nation' or to be destined to lead humankind on the road of progress, justice, etc.) Nothing is more clearly particularistic in this sense than institutional claims of universality.

The true universalistic element, however, lies in the *internal* process of individualization: virtual deconstruction and reconstruction of primary identities. And it is all the more effective when it has been achieved through difficult and violent conflicts, where oppression and revolt have threatened the hegemonic structure with internal collapse. 'Individualized individuals' do not exist by nature: they are created through the conflictual (dis)integration of primary memberships – that is to say, when individuals can view the wider community as a *liberating* agency, which frees them from belonging to one single group, or possessing a single, undifferentiated, massive identity. It is universalistic because, in a typical 'short circuit', it is working both *from above* and *from below* with respect to 'particular' groups and communities. Of course, the corresponding experience is by nature ambivalent: it can also – it *has to be* – lived as denaturization, 'coercion' of affective ties and natural sentiments in the name of 'Reason', of 'Shared Notions'. This is indeed exactly what ideologies and standards of education are in the business of explaining and implementing.

This process has been working since the very beginnings of state structures. It is a decisive means of integration, or community building, because it produces or enhances individual *subjectivity* – that is, both a loyalty directed towards a more abstract, or symbolic, or (in Benedict Anderson's terms) 'imagined' community, and a distance between private life and social life, individual initiative and collective duties (a 'moral', rather than 'ritual', obedience: one in which conviction and conscience are more important than custom and 'natural' authority). In my view there is no doubt that Hegel was right: 'private life' and 'private conscience' become autonomous precisely as a consequence of this subsumption and transformation of 'natural' memberships or primary 'cultures' under the law of the state, and remain tied to it. Or – to put it better – private life and conscience can become a matter of conflict between the interests of particular communities and the public interests of the state, but only because every 'subject' has *already* been distantiated from his or her immediate membership (even before his individual birth) through the existence of the state or public sphere. In modern states, this constitution of subjectivity, which is a permanent tension between memberships and citizenship, takes the form of individual property, personal choice of profession and opinions, 'free play' of alternative loyalties offered by churches, family and school, political parties and unions, or in more abstract terms, a 'complex equality', which altogether form a 'civil society', supported and loosely controlled by the state but not identified with its central apparatus, as Locke, Hegel, Tocqueville, Gramsci, and Michael Walzer have explained, each in his own way.

Fictive or total universality is effective as a means of integration – it demonstrates its own universality, so to speak – because it leads *dominated groups* to struggle against discrimination or inequality *in the very name* of the superior values of the community: the legal and ethical values of the state itself (notably: justice). This is clearly the case when, in the name of equal opportunity for all human individuals, feminist movements attack the discriminative 'patriarchal' laws and customs which protect the authoritarian structure of the male-dominated famly, while extending it to the whole professional and cultural realm. It is also the case when dominated ethnic groups or religious denominations demand equality in the name of the pluralistic or liberal values which the state officially incorporates in its constitution. And it was clearly demonstrated throughout the nineteenth and twentieth centuries by the way class struggles forced the nation-state to acknowledge specific rights of labour and incorporate them into the constitutional order. The process was 'Marxist', but the result was 'Hegelian'. By taking part in the organized class struggle (and first of all by imposing their right to 'join forces' against exploitation), workers ceased to form a simple dominated 'internally excluded' mass; they individualized themselves, and created new mediations for the state. To confront the hegemonic structure by denouncing the gap or contradiction between its official values and its actual practice – with greater or lesser success – is the most effective way of enforcing its universality.

Now we should not forget the counterpart of this form of universality: it is indeed *normalization*. This, of course, is where things become more ambiguous. Hegemony liberates the individual from immediate membership, but which individual? It requires and develops subjectivity, but which subjectivity? One which is compatible with normality. Within the boundaries of fictive universality, a free individual (enjoying freedom of conscience and initiative, and also, in a more material sense, such liberties as possession of personal belonging, a right to privacy, and a right to speak on the public stage, to be educationally and professionally competitive, and so on) has to be 'normal' in several senses. He or she has to be mentally healthy, that is, to conform to ways of reasoning and private behaviour which do not disturb the standard patterns of communication. He or she has to conform to the dominant sexual patterns (or, if this is not the case, to hide his or her sexual habits, therefore leading a schizophrenic existence; or, in the very 'best' circumstances, to live them openly, albeit in the framework of some stigmatized 'subculture').[5] He or she has to be moral or conscientious and, of course, obey the legal rules against criminal behaviour. In saying all this, I am not taking a moral stance *pro* or *contra* the existence of the normal subject, I am simply reiterating that normality is the standard price to be paid for the universalistic liberation of the individual from immediate subjection to primary communities. For normality is not the simple fact of adopting customs and obeying rules or laws: it means internalizing representations of the 'human type' or the 'human subject' (not exactly an essence, but a norm and a standard way of behaving) in order to be recognized as a person in one's own right – to become *presentable* (fit to be seen) in order to be represented. To become *responsible* (fit to be answered) in order to be respected.

This allows us to understand why the key structures of hegemony – the deep structures of 'hegemonic' reason – are always family structures, educational and judicial institutions: not so much because they inculcate dominant opinions or maintain authoritarian traditions, but because they immediately display the symbolic patterns of normality and responsibility in everyday life: the normal sexual difference and complementarity of genders, the normal hierarchy of intellectual capacities and models of rational discourse, the normal distinction between honesty and criminality, or between fair and illegal ways of acquiring power and wealth (in short, what the moral tradition called 'natural law'). This is not to say that in a 'normal' society everybody is 'normal', or that there is no deviance or hypocrisy, but that anyone who is not 'normal' has to be segregated or repressed or excluded, or to hide himself or herself, or to play a double game one way or another. This is the latent condition which allows otherness or difference to become integrated within a 'total' ideology or hegemony. It also reveals what remains the internal obsession of every hegemony: neither the simple fact of conflicts, not even radical social antagonisms, however threatening they can be for the ruling classes; nor, on the other hand, the existence of 'deviant' groups, or 'radical movements' directed against moral and cultural norms, but, rather, the combination of both which takes place whenever individuality can be claimed only on condition of challenging the social forms (or rules) of normality. But this leads me to examine another concept of universality, which I call *ideal universality*.

Universality as a Symbol

Again, some misunderstandings should be avoided here. Instead of 'symbolic', perhaps I should say 'ideal' or 'idealistic' universality, because what is at stake is not another degree of fiction. It is, rather, the fact that universality also exists *as an ideal*, in the form of absolute or infinite claims which are symbolically raised against the limits of any institution.

Perhaps it should be suggested that, in fact, 'fictive' universality could never exist without a latent reference to 'ideal' universality or, as Jacques Derrida might put it, some *spectre* which can never be deconstructed. Justice as an institution may not only require that subjectivity be formed when individuals 'internalize' common or universal values. It may also require, at a deeper level, to be rooted in some open or latent *insurrection*, which gave subjectivity its 'infinite' character or (against every form of social status) equated it with a quest for 'absolute' liberty.

In Marxist terms, this would be the problem of how dominant ideologies are constituted with respect to the 'consciousness' of dominant and dominated people. Marx's original formulation (in *The German Ideology*), asserting that 'the dominant ideology is always the ideology of the dominant class', is hardly tenable: not only does it make ideology a mere duplicate or reflection of economic power (thus making it impossible to understand how 'ideological' domination can contribute to 'real' domination, or add something to it), but precludes the possibility of explaining how any social *consent* or *consensus* can be forced, except by trick, mystification, deception, and so on – that is, catgories borrowed from a fantasmatic psychology. The alternative seems to be to reverse the pattern, and propose the (only apparently) paradoxical idea that the necessary condition for an ideology to become dominant is that it should elaborate the values and claims of the 'social majority', become the discourse of *the dominated* (distorted or inverted as it may appear). 'Society', or the dominant forces in society, can speak to the masses in the language of universalistic values (rights, justice, equality, welfare, progress . . .), because in this language a kernel remains which came from the masses themselves, and is returned to them.

This formulation, however, certainly does not eliminate every mystery, if only because the authentic discourse of the dominated, 'prior' to any hegemonic use, cannot be isolated as such. It appears mainly as a 'forgotten' origin, or is testified to not so much by actual words as by practical resistance, the irreducible 'being there' of the dominated. . . . The actual relationship between dominant and dominated in the field of ideology must remain ambivalent in history, but there is undoubtedly a meaning of universality which is intrinsically linked with the notion of *insurrection*, in the broad sense ('insurgents' are those who collectively rebel against domination in the name of freedom and equality). This meaning I call *ideal universality* – not only because it supports all the idealistic philosophies which view the course of history as a general process of emancipation, a realization of the idea of man (or the human essence, or the classless society, etc.), but because it introduces the notion of *the unconditional* into the realm of politics.

A crucial example – perhaps the only one, if we admit that it could be formulated several times in different places and epochs, and in different words – is the proposition concerning human rights which is expressed in the classical 'bourgeois' eighteenth-century Declarations or Bills. More precisely, it is the proposition which reverses the traditional relationship between subjection and citizenship, and justifies the universal extension of political (civic) rights (or the general equivalence of 'citizen' and 'man', in classical terminology), by explaining that *equality and liberty are inseparable* – in some sense identical – notions. I call this proposition 'equaliberty' [*égaliberté*], after an old Roman formula [*aequa libertas*] which has never ceased to haunt political philospohy in modern times, from Tocqueville to Rawls (see Balibar 1994). What is striking here is that equaliberty is an all-or-nothing notion: it cannot be relativized, according to historical or cultural conditions, but it is there or it is not there, it is recognized or ignored (as a principle – or better, as a demand).

Again, universality in this sense has both an extensive and an intensive aspect. The extensive aspect lies in the fact that human rights cannot be limited or restricted in their application: there is an inherent contradiction in the idea that not every human being enjoys rights which are constitutive of humanity. Hence the proselytic or expansive aspect of the ideal of equaliberty (which, as a discourse, can cover very different practices). Expansion can be interpreted in a geographical sense, but above all in a sociological one, meaning that no group is 'by nature' outside the claim of rights. Of course, this is all the more revealing when, in political, social or domestic institutions, certain 'categories' or 'classes' are relegated to minority status, while the principle itself remains asserted: workers, women, slaves or servants, foreigners, 'minorities' in general. But this brings us to the *intensive* aspect, which is the really decisive one.

I think that this intensive universality can be identified with the *critical* effect of any discourse in which it is stated that equality and liberty are not distinct concepts, or that a 'contradiction' opposing the requisites of liberty and of equality is ruled out in principle (they therefore do not have to be 'reconciled' through the institution of a preferential order or a reciprocal limitation). In more practical terms, *if* no equality can be achieved without liberty, *then* the reverse is also true: no liberty can be achieved without equality.[6]

Such a proposition is dialectical by nature. It undoubtedly has a positive content: to indicate that freedom and equality will proceed *pari passu* (remain blocked or progress) in 'cities' or societies, be they national or transnational. It can, however, be shown to be true or absolutely justified only *negatively*, by refuting its own negations (or by displaying its internal negativity): this amounts to defining 'liberty' or freedom as *non-coercion*, and equality or 'parity' as *non-discrimination*, both notions being open to various definitions according to ancient and novel experiences of constraint and discrimination. The proposition then becomes: abolishing or fighting discrimination also implies abolishing or fighting constraint and coercion. In this sense, the 'insurrectional' content of ideal universality becomes manifest.

From this negativity follows the intersubjective – or, better, transindividual – character of ideal universality. Rights to equality and liberty are indeed *individual*: only individuals can claim and support them. But the abolition of both coercion and discrimination (which we may call emancipation) is always clearly a *collective process*, which can be achieved only if many individuals (virtually all of them) unite and join forces against oppression and social inequality. In other words, equaliberty is never something that can be *bestowed* or *distributed*; it has to be won. There is a direct connection here with what Hannah Arendt called 'a right to acquire rights', as distinct from enjoying this or that already existing right which is guaranteed by law. The 'right to rights' clearly is not (or not primarily) a moral notion; it is a political one. It describes a process which started with resistance and ends in the actual exercise of a 'constituent power', whichever particular historical form this may take. It should therefore also be called a *right to politics*, in the broad sense, meaning that nobody can be properly emancipated from outside or from above, but only by his or her own (collective) activity. This is precisely what rebels or insurgents from various democratic revolutions in the past have claimed (what they are still claiming, if there are revolutions in our own time).

Let me press the point that such a concept of universality is *ideal* – which is not to say that it does not play an active role (or that there are no processes of emancipation). What we observe, rather, is that the ideal of non-discrimination and non-coercion is 'immortal' or irrepressible, that it is revived again and again in different situations, but also that it has shifted continually throughout history. We all know that, although the American and French Revolutions declared that *all men* (meaning: human beings) were 'free and equal by birthright', the resulting social and political orders were permeated with a number of restrictions, discriminations, and authoritarian aspects, beginning with the exclusion of women and wage-labourers from full citizenship. In short, they were clearly contradictory with respect to their own universalistic principles.[7] Moreover, the slogans of the workers' movement, at the beginning, were a revival of equaliberty, or the universal right to politics. Suffice it here to remember the phrases in the Inaugural Address of the First International (1864): 'the emancipation of the working classes must be conquered by the working classes themselves'.

But the clearest modern example is the feminist or women's liberation movement, which is *also* a movement for equality, arising from the evidence that a paternalistic or protective granting of rights and opportunities to women by the will of men is a contradiction in terms.[8] As a consequence, it is not simply a 'political movement' (with ethical and social dimensions), it is also a transformation of politics in essence, or a transformation of the *relationship* between genders which is reflected in existing political practice.

An emancipatory movement in this sense has a symbolic and

universalistic dimension *per se*: although at first it mobilizes members of the oppressed group, it can achieve its goals only if it becomes a general movement, if it aims at changing the whole fabric of society. Inasmuch as women struggling for parity transform resistance into politics, they are not trying to win particular rights for a 'community', which would be the 'community of women'. From the emancipatory standpoint, *gender is not a community*. Or perhaps I should say that the only gender which is a community is the masculine, inasmuch as males establish institutions and develop practices to protect old privileges (and I should add: by doing so, males virtually transform 'political society' into an affective community, where processes of identification can take place).[9] As Susan Wolf rightly argues, there is nothing like a 'women's culture' in this sense in which anthropologists talk about the culture of a community (be it ethnic or social/professional). On the other hand, however, *every* community is structured around a certain form of relationship between genders, specific forms of sexual, affective, and economic subjection. Hence it must be recognized that the position of women (both the 'real' position in the division of activities and distribution of powers, and the 'symbolic' position which is presented in discourse) is a structural element which determines the character of every culture, be it the culture of a particular group, a social movement, or a whole society with its inherited civilization.

Women's struggle for parity, therefore, being a complex struggle for non-differentition within non-discrimination, creates a *solidarity* (or achieves citizenship) without creating a *community*. In Jean-Claude Milner's terms, women are typically a 'paradoxical class': neither united by the imaginary of resemblance, of 'natural' kinship, nor called by some symbolic voice, which would allow them to view themselves as an 'elect' group. Rather, this struggle virtually transforms the community. It is therefore immediately universalistic, and this allows us to imagine that it could transform the very notion of politics, including forms of authority and representation, which suddenly appear particularistic (not to speak of the forms of nationhood, including their typical connection with warfare).

I think that this kind of argument has a critical impact on

discussions about 'minorities' 'minority rights', and also – at least indirectly – 'multiculturalism' and cultural conflicts. The ambivalent story of conjunctural unity and long-term divergences between the emancipatory struggles of women and the movements of national, ethnic or cultural liberation (not to speak of religious revival) has never, to my knowledge, been written in a comprehensive manner. The contradictions are not less important here than they were (and are) between working-class struggle and feminism, especially where the former has become a defensive movement which aims at protecting a 'working-class culture' within the broader framework of national hegemony.

This, however, should not lead us to simplistic conclusions. On the one hand, we should admit that the contradiction is not merely empirical, or accidental. It is a contradiction in the principles themselves. As a consequence, we should not keep using such notions as 'minority' and 'difference' in a manner which is itself undifferentiated. If women are a 'minority', this cannot be in the same sense as cultural, religious and ethnic minorities. If they are considered to be the 'majority', or to represent the interests of the majority in a given period, this cannot be in the same sense in which, when I was discussing 'real universality', I said that new transnational cultures are becoming potentially majoritarian in a world of increasing migrations and mixtures.

On the other hand, however, this recognition of the inner tension between 'differences' which lies at the root of many disappointing results of utopian discourses about the 'new citizenship' cannot lead us to the proposition that 'cultural' struggles, expressing a demand for autonomy, or recognition, or equality of communities which have long been excluded from political representation, and are still torn between opposing politics of exclusion and assimilation (like communities of migrants), are *particularistic* by their very nature. According to circumstances, they can have a universalistic component, clearly, in all the three directions which I have been examining. From the point of view of *real universality*, first, because they can play a direct role in challenging the 'internal exclusion' on a world scale that continuously re-creates racism. From the point of view of *fictive universality*, second, because they can constitute a struggle for broadening the spectrum of pluralism, and therefore *expanding subjectivity*, or challenging the ways of life and thought which have raised above society the self-image of some historically privileged group, under the name of 'reason'. From the point of view of *ideal universality*, finally, because discrimination between cultures (not only class cultures, but also ethnic cultures from West and East, North and South, etc.) is usually also (and perhaps first and foremost) a way of reproducing intellectual difference and hierarchies, or a *de facto* privileging of those men, women, and above all children, who are more 'congenial' to established standards of communication. This is something which has always been conflictual in national societies (with their colonial and imperial dependencies), but it becomes truly explosive in a transnational environment. Once again we realize that in politics there are realities, fictions and ideals, but there are no essences.

The threefold meaning of universality which I have described is aporetic (at least, so it seems to me). There is no 'final answer'. But each point can have some practical implications.

I distinguished, in a somewhat Lacanian way, three instances of universality: *universality as reality*, *universality as fiction*, and *universality as a symbol (or an ideal)*. They are never isolated, independent of one another, but they remain irreducible, and make sense in different realms.

Real universality is a process which creates a single 'world' by multiplying the interdependencies between the units – be they economic, political or cultural – that form the network of social activities today. What is now called 'globalization' is only the backlash of an age-old process, constantly fostered by capitalist expansion, which started with the constitution of rival national units, at least in the core of the world-economy. They are still with us today – very much so – but they can no longer provide models for the world-scale institutions and community-building processes now on the horizon. I suggested that this has not only political but also philosophical consequences, because it renders obsolete the classical cosmopolitan utopias which relied upon the idea of a spiritual realm *beyond* state institutions, since these intellectual constructions have now been virtually overtaken by real universalization itself. Above all, I insisted on two points. *First*, that globalization exacerbates minority status, but at the same time makes it more difficult for a growing number of individuals or groups to become classified within *simple* denominations of identities. *Second*, that the immediate – and probably lasting – effect of the blurring of borders between nations, empires, and former 'blocs' is a dramatic increase in interethnic or pseudo-ethnic conflicts, mainly expressed and stereotyped in cultural terms. I could rephrase the whole thing by saying that in this context *identities* are more than ever used as *strategies*, both defensive and aggressive, and this means imposing such identities both upon others and upon oneself. The kind of strategies we are confronted with could not be understood if we did not constantly remember that the play of difference is underpinned and overdetermined by the general pattern of *inequalities*, both old (notably those coming from colonialism and imperialism) and *new* inequalities, arising from the at least partial disintegration of national-social states. As a consequence, the politics of identity or the strategies of identity-defence are ultimately means of resisting inequality, or universality as inequality. But the reverse is also true: we cannot imagine that the struggle against inequalities in a 'globalized' world will ever solve the problem of cultural diversity, and therefore put an end to resistance to uniformization and homogenization. How can we *universalize resistance* without *reinforcing* the insistence on exclusive identity and otherness which the system already produces and instrumentalizes?

There is no 'given' theoretical solution to this riddle. We may very cautiously imagine that the practical solution arises progressively from the fact that *not all cultural diversities are ethnic*. There are indeed new, post-ethnic or post-national, cultural identities emerging, just as there are old cultural identities reviving (e.g. religious). We may also derive hope from the fact that *diversities other than cultural* are competing with them in the self-identification of individuals (above all, gender identities and sexual diversities: there are excellent indications of this in Connolly).

The other two concepts of universality which I distinguished are *fictive universality* and *ideal universality*. By fictive universality I mean the kind of universality which was involved in the constitution of social *hegemonies*, and therefore always based upon the existence of state institutions, be they traditional and religious, or modern and secular. The ambivalence of universality here takes the form of a typical combination (as Hegel would say) between the liberation of *individual* subjectivity from narrow communitarian bonds, and the imposition of a *normal* – that is, normative and normalized – pattern of individual behaviour. I stressed the fact that although – or, rather, because – this is *constructed*, there is a true element of universality here: namely, the fact that a political hegemony, which in the modern world has taken the 'secular' form of *national* citizenship, creates the possibility for individuals to *escape* the 'impossible' oscillation or contradiction between two impossible extremes: an absolute reduction of personal identity to *one* role or membership, and a permanent floating – we might call it postmodern – between multiple contingent identities offered by the 'cultural market'. But the very high price to be paid for that (some believe they pay it easily; others become aware of the real cost) is not only normality, but also exclusion: in the form of both internal exclusion – suppression of one's own desires and potential – and external exclusion – suppression of deviant behaviour and groups. There is no doubt in my mind that the kind of *substantial* collective identity which is created by the functioning of hegemonic institutions (what I have called *fictitive ethnicity* in the case of the nation-state, or an imaginary community *beyond* 'private' or 'particular' membership [see Balibar and Wallerstein]) is a key structure of the whole system of normalization and exclusion, precisely because it is (or was once) a powerful instrument for opening a space for liberties, especially in the form of social struggles and democratic demands. Hence the permanent tension of this historical form of citizenship. Now the crucial problem emerges precisely when the process of globalization makes it progressively more impossible to organize hegemony (purely) within the national framework, or requires, if democracy is to be preserved or reconstructed, that it take post-national or transnational forms. We should not underestimate the fact that this is the main reason why fictive universality in this sense regresses towards particularism, or *national* identity virtually *loses* its 'hegemonic' character – its (even limited) pluralist capacities – to become another form of *one-dimensional* identity.

Finally, I called *ideal universality* the subversive element which the philosophers called *negativity*. It may have been necessary to *ground* any political hegemony historically on the experience of revolution in the broad sense, or popular insurrection. But on the other hand, such a negativity goes *beyond* any institutional citizenship, by posing the infinite question of equality *and* liberty together, or the impossibility of actually achieving freedom *without* equality, or equality *without* liberty. I insisted on the fact that such an ideal of universality, which has emerged again and again throughout history (and therefore seems to be irrepressible), is *transindividual by nature*. It is a question not of speaking the established language of politics, of 'playing the game' according to its well-known rules, but of collectively breaking through the limits of public communication by means of a new language. The best examples in this sense are those of the 'paradoxical classes' which claim the rights of a 'particular' group not in the name of this very peculiarity, but because its discrimination or exclusion appears to involve a negation of human universality as such: the classical *proletariat*, and *women*, engaged in a movement for parity or equality-in-difference. I do not exclude the possibility that other social movements have a universal component in this sense – that is, aim at removing some universal discrimination by asserting the rights of (and to) some fundamental difference. But I want to emphasize that there is no pre-established harmony between such different 'ideals', although each of them undoubtedly embodies one aspect of universality. Possibly we should admit that in a very deep sense (affecting the very notion of 'humankind'), the *ideal universal* is *multiple* by nature – not in the sense of being 'relative', less than unconditional, bound to compromise, but, rather, in the sense of being always-already beyond any simple or 'absolute' unity, and therefore a permanent source of conflict. This has obvious practical consequence, notably the non-existence of any spontaneous or 'natural' force of heterogeneous 'minorities' against the dominant universality, or the 'system' as such. This in turn does not mean that unity (or common goals) cannot be constructed in given circumstances. But here we come back to the question of choice, and the *risk or finitude of choice*, which I mentioned when I was discussing the ambivalence of ideals. It is the same problem. Philosophy can give a name to it, but philosophy cannot solve it.

Notes

This essay is an abridged and slightly revised version of the paper presented on 18 February 1994 at the Conference 'Cultural Diversities: On Democracy, Community and Citizenship', The Bohen Foundation, New York. An amended and expanded version was published in Étienne Balibar, *La Crainte des masses. Politique et philosophie avant et après Marx* (Paris: Galilée, 1997).

1. This was also part of the lesson taught by such anthropologists as Roger Bastide a generation ago.

2. As laid out in his *Lectures on the Philosophy of History*, and mainly his *Philosophy of Right*, 3rd Part (§§142–360).

3. This is not to say that there are no movements in history which aim at 'messianic' identification of individual minds on a religious or national basis. But precisely these movements are 'excessive' and partial; they are hardly compatible with social 'normality' and the building of institutions in the long run – with the 'routinization of charisma', as Weber put it. On the notion of 'pluralism' as a national name for hegemony in American history, see Zunz.

4. This last case is clearly decisive: class loyalties, especially *working-class* loyalty, becomes a decisive pillar of national hegemony as soon as it is transformed into a particular 'culture' and a political 'opinion' or set of opinions *within* the political system, whose contribution to the national history or spirit is officially recognized in the (national-) social state. The ideological process of hegemonic integration transforms *difference* – that is, class antagonism – into *particularism*, a simple 'class culture': this is indeed easier when that class culture is also an ethnic or quasi-ethnic one. Hence the ambivalence of 'ethnicity' in immigration states: it is the background both of their collective resistance against exploitation, and of their integration (sometimes their desire for integration, called 'recognition') into the national unit. See Noiriel.

5. This is where a critical discussion of the *opposite effects* of 'real universality' and 'fictive universality' is very relevant: 'subcultures and 'deviant behaviour' can be valorized by the market, in given economic conditions, whereas they are always stigmatized by 'hegemonic' state morals. For twenty years now, the USA has been a fascinating arena for this contradiction.

6. Of course, I choose these terms to show the opposition between this

conception of universality – which, I think, is a constant in the interpretation of democracy as 'insurrection', both from the English-American and the French point of view – and the 'problem' from which John Rawls deduces his revised theory of justice in recent writings. He would certainly not deny the opposition himself. However, whether Kant's philosophy stands completely on one side of the debate might be less easy to decide.

7. This contradiction had its collective counterpart in revolts or 'conspiracies', but also its subjective result in 'madness': see Roudinesco.

8. For the combination of liberty and equality inasmuch as it concerns the relationship between genders in society – that is, has a political meaning – some French feminists use the term 'parity'.

9. This in turn requires that they impose disciplinary sexual roles not only upon others, but also upon themselves: 'normality', the figure of political power is homosexual; the figure of family bond is heterosexual. Whether a political society which is not a community can exist, and what form the 'play' of affects would take there, remains a very mysterious question.

References

Anderson, Benedict (1985) *Imagined Communities: Reflections on the Origin and Spread of Nationalism.* London: Verso.

Arendt, Hannah (1968) *Imperialism.* New York: Harcourt.

Balibar, Étienne (1994) *Masses, Classes, Ideas: Studies on Politics and Philosophy before and after Marx.* New York: Routledge.

Balibar, Étienne and Immanueal Wallerstein (1991) *Race, Nation, Class: Ambiguous Identities.* London: Verso.

Bastide, Roger (1967) *Les Amériques Noires.* Paris: Payot.

—— (1971) *Antaropologie appliquée.* Paris: Payot.

Connolly, William E. (1991) *Identity/Difference: Democratic Negotiations of Political Paradox.* Ithaca, NY: Cornell University Press.

Derrida, Jacques (1994) *Specters of Marx*, trans. Peggy Kamuf. New York and London: Routledge.

Gellner, Ernest (1987) *Culture, Identity, and Politics.* Cambridge: Cambridge University Press.

Gonzalez Casanova, Pablo (1995) 'Ciudadanos, Proletarios y Pueblos: El Universalismo Hoy.' *L'avenir des idéologies, les idéologies d l'avenir.* Paris: Maison des Sciences de l'Homme.

Hegel, Georg Wilhelm Freidrich (1991) *Elements of the Philiosophy of Right*, trans. H.B. Nisbett. Cambridge: Cambridge University Press.

Kant, Immanuel (1784/1990) 'What is Enlightenment?' in *Political Writings*, trans. H.B. Nisbett. Cambridge: Cambridge University Press.

Milner, Jean-Claude (1985) *Les Noms indistincts.* Paris: Seuil.

Noirel, Gérard (1984) *Longwy: Immigrés et prolétaires (1880–1980)*. Paris: Presses Universitaires de France.

Rawls, John (1993) *Political Liberalism*. New York: Columbia University Press.

Roudinesco Élisabeth (1992) *Théroigne de Méricourt*, trans. M.A. Thom. London: Verso.

Taylor, Charles (1992) *Multiculturalism and 'The Politics of Recognition'*. Princeton, NJ: Princeton University Press.

Wallerstein, Immanuel (1991) *Geopolitics and Geoculture: Essays on a Changing World-System*. Cambridge: Cambridge University Press.

Wolf, Susan (1992) 'Comment', in Taylor, *Multiculturalism and 'The Politics of Recognition'*, pp. 75–85.

Zunz, Olivier (1987) 'Genèse du pluralisme américain', *Annales E.S.c.2*: pp. 429–44.